THEME

and Variations

My Life's Journey

MICHAEL MIROPOLSKY

Foreword by Melinda Bargreen

THEME and Variations, *My Life's Journey*
by Michael Miropolsky

Copyright © 2016 Michael Miropolsky
First edition
Published by Michael Miropolsky

Editors: Melinda Bargreen, Josie Solseng, Evelina Miropolsky
Design by Ellen Lund
Front cover photo by Eric Linger
Back cover photo by Larey McDaniel
Photos included in this book also were taken by Leonid Keylin
        and Veronica Ho.
Printed by CreateSpace
Printed in the United States of America

ISBN: 1533395993
EAN: 978-1533395993

To my children, my best creation in this life:
Evelina, Alex, and Yulia.

Acknowledgements

Many people have contributed greatly to my book. In this brief acknowledgement I would like to thank at least a few of them.

MELINDA BARGREEN, an extraordinary writer, for her enthusiastic support, generous assistance, and over two decades of friendship.

ELLEN LUND, a unique artist, who also designed the art for most of my CDs, as well the book *Measures and Pleasures,* and who always surprises me with fresh artistic discoveries in our projects together.

JOSIE SOLSENG, whose sharp eye did not allow even the smallest discrepancies in my writing. I learned a lot from our collaboration.

EVELINA, my daughter, who as an editor has brought her great writing skills to help me with this project, who revised and refined with great patience what I thought was already perfect.

ALEX, my son, for helping me organize a lot of the book's material and for contributing his outstanding computer skills, an area in which I often feel quite handicapped.

LIZA PLOTKIN, my loyal partner for almost a decade, for her incredible patience and encouragement.

MY PARENTS, for directing their silly seven-year-old boy into music, and for setting the best example of how to raise my own children.

MY SISTER, for her unconditional love.

ZINAIDA and SEMYON TREYGER, GENRICH and NELLY SIVORI-NOVSKY, and LEONID and TATYANA KEYLIN, for their kind hearts, deep friendship, and mentorship in the American chapter of my life.

MY GENEROUS DONORS AND PATRONS, who over the years have supported my artistic endeavors.

vi

Because of my profession as a violinist and conductor, there are so many people who have touched my life, and *thanks* to my profession as a violinist and a conductor, I have been able to touch the lives of many others. Some of them have had a direct and powerful influence on me while others remain unnamed, but all of them have left a part of themselves with me, helping to create the person I am today.

Without you there would be no me. Without you there would be no book.

Thank you!

Michael Miropolsky

Foreword by Melinda Bargreen

The story you are about to read is an extraordinary one by any standard: a saga of great talent and perseverance overcoming the most daunting political odds, hardships, personal tragedies, and obstacles of every kind. But then, Michael Miropolsky is an extraordinary person. His love of music and his great talent have brought him from the oppressive regime of the former Soviet Union to Seattle, where he has become not only a mainstay of the Seattle Symphony Orchestra, but also the creator of several new musical ensembles. Furthermore, Miropolsky has taken up the conductor's baton as well as his lifelong companion, the violin, and he is now music director of several local and regional symphony orchestras – an important and influential figure in the Pacific Northwest music world.

Miropolsky's life story is full of wit and humor, and it also is a rarely heard insider's account of life in Kyrgyzstan (and, later, in Moscow) during the Soviet era. His colorful writing style is all the more impressive when you reflect that English is not his mother tongue. Miropolsky's ruminations on playing the violin and on becoming a conductor will put you inside the orchestra and on the podium in a direct, "you are there" manner. Frank, witty, and full of thoughtful detail, this is a memoir to savor, and one that will make you think.

—Melinda Bargreen

Music critic, The Seattle Times (1977-2008); freelance writer for the Times, Classical KING FM, the American Record Guide, and other publications; author of the books "50 Years of Seattle Opera" and "Classical Seattle: Maestros, Impresarios, Virtuosi, and Other Music Makers."

CONTENTS

Introduction xiii

PART ONE: RUSSIA

Prelude 3

Chapter 1. House 7

Chapter 2. Frunze 11

Chapter 3. Central Market 19

Chapter 4. My Parents 22

Chapter 5. UFO 26

Chapter 6. Music School 28

Chapter 7. Moscow 34

Chapter 8. The Mausoleum 39

Chapter 9. Gnessin Special School of Music 41

Chapter 10. Gnessin State Musical College 51

Chapter 11. Military Ensemble: Private Mikhail 66

Interlude: The Heat 70

Chapter 12. My First Marriage 71

Chapter 13. The Bolshoi Theatre 73

Chapter 14. Moscow State Symphony Orchestra 76

Chapter 15. Tours Abroad 81

Chapter 16. Quartet 87

Chapter 17. The Decline of the Golden Era 93

Chapter 18. Conductors and Their Orchestras 100

Chapter 19. My New Place 107

Chapter 20. Larisa 108

Chapter 21. Silent Revolution 112

Chapter 22. Emigration 114

Photo Album: Russia 117

PART TWO: AMERICA

Prelude: Musical Diaspora 127

Chapter 23. San Francisco 129

Chapter 24. Evelina 132

Chapter 25. First Car 136

Chapter 26. Zoya and Leon 137

Chapter 27. Auditions 140

Chapter 28. Fake Italian 143

Chapter 29. The Apartment 144

Chapter 30. Our American Dream 146

Chapter 31. Movie Recordings 148

Chapter 32. Seattle Symphony Orchestra 150

Chapter 33. Orchestra People 154

Chapter 34. The Other Side of the Coin 156

Chapter 35. Citizenship 159

Interlude: What is Success? 161

Chapter 36. Seattle Conservatory of Music 162

Chapter 37. Seattle Violin Virtuosi 165

Chapter 38. Cascade Symphony Orchestra 168

Chapter 39. Family Travels 175

Chapter 40. Children 184

Chapter 41. BPO, LWSO, TSO 186

Chapter 42. Violin versus Baton 189

Chapter 43. Seattle: The Northwest City 198

Chapter 44. Cloudy 200

Chapter 45. Auer, Reuven and Jascha 202

Chapter 46. Jean-Baptiste Vuillaume 205

Chapter 47. Sticks with Horsehair 208

Chapter 48. The John and Carmen Delo Assistant Principal
                Second Violin 211

Chapter 49. Tragedy 213

Chapter 50. Remarkable Memories 216

Chapter 51. Concert: Tchaikovsky's Fifth 223

Chapter 52. A "Master" Around Every Corner 226

Eternity 229

Closing Note 231

Maestro, Play On - by Dale Burrows 232

Photo Album: America 235

Introduction

I have chosen this title, *THEME and Variations*, for my book because music is the theme of my life, with numerous variations that accompany it in their own ways. It is also the name of one of my most favorite musical compositions, Bach's *Chaconne* for solo violin. It's an immortal piece, simple in its musical idea, but touched by the hand of a genius to become a rare human achievement. I am not ashamed to admit that one of the few times in my life that brought me to tears was when I heard Jascha Heifetz playing that *Chaconne*. My theme is music, my variations are time and places and people.

I started writing my story on my 60th birthday. You are holding my biggest dream in your hands and I am very happy that it has come true. My dream was to write a book about my life, which may sound egotistical, but I assure you there is not a drop of ego in this project. This is my way of introducing my life to my kids, who know almost nothing about me, as well as to my numerous friends in the audience and in the orchestras with which I work. I wish I could share this dream with my parents, but my heart is happy knowing that they would be proud of me.

When my father turned 60, I was 17 years old. He appeared to me a very old man, so old that I could not imagine myself ever being that age. And yet here I am, and I am pretty sure that in the eyes of most 17 year olds, I am that terribly old man. I don't know how my father felt when he was 60, but I don't feel older than 40, and people say that is a good sign.

When I turned 60, I felt ready to comb through my life from the beginning, ready to tell the story about the little boy digging in the dirt in his backyard and collecting worms in his shirt pocket and about his exciting and eventful transformation into the man I am to-day. I hope you enjoy reading about my journey as much as I enjoyed writing it.

"Writing a book is an adventure. To begin with it is a toy and an amusement. Then it becomes a mistress, then it becomes a master, then it becomes a tyrant".
—*Winston S. Churchill*

PART ONE: RUSSIA

Prelude

I was born in Frunze, Kyrgyzstan, USSR in 1955, but I will start my story further back in time. My parents' families had been part of a fairly large Jewish community in Ukraine for as long as they could remember, and nobody could say exactly when the Miropolskys and Krasilovskys (my mother's maiden name) came to Ukraine to settle.

Piotr Miropolsky (my father) and Faina Krasilovsky (my mother) knew each other from childhood. Their families shared a one-level house (similar to a modern duplex) in the small town of Szibulev. Their fathers fought on the fields of the First World War, and came back alive. My grandfather on my father's side was severely injured. He lost a few ribs, and limped from an injury, but remained physically very strong. After the war, he worked at a sugar factory. There was never enough food in those days, and once a week all employees of the factory received a bonus: two kilograms of sugar. My father was allowed to take half and bring it to Faina's family. That was his modest chance to say a few words to Faina. Their weekly "sugar dates" went on for a while and soon Piotr was crazy in love with Faina. He proposed and she accepted. The wedding was not fancy, but they were happy. Soon my father got a job at a school as a history teacher. Faina started working as a secretary in the construction business. Piotr was so much in love with his beautiful young wife that he could not wait for her to come back home after work every day. He would sit in his chair, waiting for her and get nervous if (by his estimate) she was late. When she came home just a few minutes later than usual he would get jealous. His jealousy would go so far that a few times he threatened to leave her, but he never followed through. At some point Faina got tired of such jealous suspicions and one night when Piotr said that he was leaving, she said, "I don't believe you." At that moment it appeared that Piotr really would leave. He had collected his belongings in a suitcase and had walked up to the door, but did not open it. Instead he sat on the suitcase and started to cry. He loved his wife so much but could not overcome the poisonous feeling in his chest. Jealousy was making him blind. Over the years he relaxed and settled down. They had three kids, and lived together for more than 50 years.

Their family names sound very pretty to the Russian ear. Miropolsky is a name combining *mir*, which means peace, and *Polsky*, meaning Polish (but nobody has any idea where the second part came from, since we don't have any Polish roots). The name Krasilovsky has at its root *krasi*, which comes from *krasiviy*, meaning beautiful. Peace and beauty – that was not a bad combination for a start.

In 1941, Nazi Germany started the war against Russia, which was to become the bloodiest event in the history of mankind. My father, like almost every man in the Soviet Union at that time, went to war to defend his country. Soon after the Nazi invasion it became clear that Hitler planned to occupy Ukraine, and according to his ideology, all Jews had to be exterminated like cockroaches. But not every Jew wanted to believe in such a monstrous truth, including a few members of my parents' families. They were so attached to their land where they were born that they refused to move to a safer place and risk losing everything they had created during decades of hard labor. They greeted the Germans with the hope that they would allow them to survive. Because of this tragic mistake, I never knew my grandparents.

In the first few days after German troops came to Szibulev where my parents lived, all Jews were monstrously murdered. In such a small town everybody knew everybody, and people knew who was Ukrainian and who was a Jew. My grandparents were buried alive, standing with their heads sticking above the ground, miserable and frightened, but breathing. On command, a designated German soldier started smashing their heads with a shovel, eventually cutting their heads from their bodies. The detached heads lay on the ground for days.

My father had already gone to war, leaving behind his pregnant wife. Just two weeks before that slaughter, my mother collected the few belongings she could carry and barely made it to the last train departing from their little town. The train was heading south where people hoped that the Germans would not reach, and where there would be some food. Hunger had become devastating in Ukraine. The fields had been abandoned and destroyed as people ran from the Nazis.

Traveling by train from Ukraine to Kyrgyzstan in this century would probably take three days. It's a big stretch of more than 2,000 miles. The trip my mother took lasted almost 100 days. She and other people were lucky to find a place on an open platform train car, packed like herring in a can. It is hard to imagine the magnitude of that exodus. Thousands and thousands of people could not make it to the trains, and were left behind. Many were Jews, since there was a big community of Jewish people in Ukraine in those days. Those who did not flee were killed.

The worst, as my mother later told me, was when German airplanes would attack the train. The Germans did not care that there were only civilians on the train. During airstrikes, the train would usually stop so people could jump off the platform, run, and hide somewhere in the bushes. My pregnant mother could not run. After each attack, a few dead bodies were thrown off the car and the train continued on its way. My mother was very lucky to have not been injured or killed.

After surviving this harrowing journey, she ended up in the capital of Kyrgyzstan, which was a part of the Russian empire called the USSR, the Union of Soviet Socialist Republics. When the train pulled into the station in Frunze it was infected with fleas and everyone aboard was forced to burn their clothes. One of the locals kindly gave my mother an old dress that became her only one for the next couple of years. When the baby was born, a cardboard box served him as a crib. The poverty of the time was indescribable.

Despite the lack of food due to rationing and other difficulties of the time, Valery was a healthy and active child. My parents soon discovered his talent for music and at age seven, Valery was accepted to a music school to study the violin. Unfortunately, he did not have enough patience for scales and exercises and dropped out after completing the sixth grade. He had a lot of physical energy that was quickly becoming a driving force in his life, and he learned to channel it into sports. Basketball became his favorite. After high school he was accepted into a college for athletes, graduated with honors, and started working as a trainer in the school.

Valery was not particularly tall, but his boundless energy and talent gained him an invitation to join the regional professional basketball team. His team started going on tour and was very successful, winning game after game. Wild parties followed each victory, and excessive drinking soon led to a foray into drug use.

Valery's life went in a bad direction, and he was unable to change its fatal course. He died tragically at the age of forty-two. The pain of his death left a wound in my parents' hearts that would remain with them for the rest of their lives.

Kyrgyzstan had a very warm climate and friendly people. The locals spoke Russian, the main language in all of the Soviet Union. Local children could not study their native language at school, just Russian. It also seemed that anti-Semitism had not yet reached Kyrgyzstan; Kyrgyz people simply did not know who the Jews were.

When the war was over there was no way back to their native land, their beloved Ukraine. The entire town my parents had lived in was flattened, and there were no remaining relatives. All roots had been cut off. My father came back after the war with a chest full of medals, a few injuries, but in one piece. His war stories would become my bedtime stories for many years to come.

Nine months after his return, my sister Larisa was born and eight years later I arrived. When I was born, I weighed barely three kilograms (just over six pounds), and was considered to be a weak baby. According to my sister, I was a cranky and stubborn child. With my Jewish luck, my June 22nd birthday matched the date of the Nazis' invasion of Russia, and the kids at school never failed to remind me of this coincidence in a very unpleasant manner. If only I'd known, I would have waited one more day! I was the youngest in the family, and in the typical Russian-Jewish tradition my parents had a lot of hopes and expectations for my future. I wasn't yet aware of this pressure since everything came quite easily to me.

1 · House

As a child, I don't recall ever having any new clothes that were bought for me, perhaps only shoes. We were very poor, as were the majority of people around us, and I wore what was passed down to me from my sister, heavily reshaped by my mother's hand to be made suitable for a boy.

My first real memory is of our house. It was divided into two parts, similar to the modern duplex, which we shared with another Jewish family. The house was built from *saman*, dried pieces of clay, which kept us warm in the winter and cool in the summer.

My mother and me in Frunze, Kyrgyzstan

Our part of the house was very small. A tiny entrance (my father had to duck to get in) led to the first room where my sister had her own bed, wedged between the window and the refrigerator. Our small dinner table could fit only two people at a time, so we took turns when it came time to eat. The room had a stove. Every day my mother created a little miracle by starting a fire in the stove. Old newspapers went on the bottom, followed by a few pieces of wood, and then charcoal to top off the pyramid. One needed to have a certain skill to deal with the stove so that the fire would last for a few hours and keep the house warm, especially in winter. If my mother was lucky the fire would start with her first attempt. It was hard and exhausting labor, and she really hated it. All our cooking was done on this stove.

The second room was slightly bigger than the first one. It contained the bed that I shared with my father, a short couch where my mother slept, a dresser, bookcase, piano, and a table with four chairs in the middle of the room. To move around, one had to sidle sideways. The bookcase contained the complete works of Vladimir Lenin. It was an excellent quality, 55-volume edition bound in dark blue. Every book was quite thick and contained around 500 pages.

I believe that many families had such a collection, and I wonder if anybody ever read all those works by the first Russian Bolshevik leader. Because he was a history teacher, my father studied some articles from that collection. He was the only one in our family who ever opened those books.

In the right corner of the very bottom shelf there was a box with old antique coins. They were all mixed together: copper, nickel, and silver. My father liked his collection, and would sometimes allow me to play with the rarities. I recall a couple of coins dating back to the 13th century, very worn out and hard to read. In another box there was a collection of old paper money. My favorite was a thick stack of uncut Russian money from 1917. It was a time when power was changing so quickly in the country that the new regime had just enough time to print the money but not enough time to cut it. Then that government would be overthrown by a new regime, which was already printing its own currency.

There were also a few porcelain dogs with very funny and unnatural faces. My father had brought them back from Germany after the war as gifts. The dogs were placed on the piano as if they were being punished, having to listen endlessly to my sister's practicing. Their shiny faces stayed still, never reacting to their torture.

In the 1960s, we had a radio with only one station. We learned about all the happy news from the socialist world and all the disastrous news from the capitalist world. In between the news, the station played Russian classical and folk music. Later, because my father was a school principal and merited the privilege, we had a telephone installed in the home.

We were proud owners of an architectural "miracle": an outdoor toilet (we did not have an indoor one). It was quite a primitive plywood box (built by my father himself) with walls, a roof, and a door. The occupant could conveniently and for understandable reasons lock the door from the inside with a small hook. The door had a hole at eye level in the shape of a diamond. I think it was there for decoration rather than for ventilation. The box sat on the ground above a hole dug approximately a meter deep. When the time would come and it was filled up, my father would cover the hole with dirt and move the toilet to a new location a couple of meters away from the old one. In summertime, using the toilet meant fighting with legions of fat and colorful flies, which we attempted to kill with chemicals but without much success. They appeared to repopulate overnight after the day's battle. In the wintertime it was amazing that nobody caught a cold; the thin walls didn't do much to shield us from the wind. The severe cold of Frunze winters made the temperature of the outhouse as freezing as it was outside. One had to learn how to do it quickly!

To get drinking water, I had to trek a couple hundred meters to the well and carry two heavy buckets filled with pure chilled water. It was my manly duty. The trick was not to splash water out on the way home. Most of the time I walked around barefoot, and one time on my errand I stepped on a big piece of glass. Strangely enough, I did not feel any pain. I carried the heavy buckets all the way back to our doorstep, leaving a bloody path on the ground behind me.

Even though our house was not big by any standards, we were lucky to have a wonderful yard lined with fruit trees. When springtime arrived we would feel like we lived in a fairytale. All the trees seemed to start blooming at the same time, creating an indescribable beauty. An ocean of intoxicating fragrance came from fifteen blooming sour cherry trees, luring dozens and dozens of bees. They would rush from one tree to the next to get as much as they could of the enticing pollen, filling their little stomachs. It was fun to watch the nonstop competition between them, as if there was some kind of reward for being the hardest working bee in the hive.

We collected as many cherries as we could; the biggest and sweetest were to be found at the treetops where they basked in the sun. My mother turned the harvest into compotes and jam, which served as our dessert all year round. My dad also contributed to the family "business," making a wonderful sweet wine from the cherries. I was allowed to taste it, and I have to admit that I liked it. Another favorite of mine was a homemade drink called *grib* (like kombucha). It was kind of a scary solution in a big glass jar. A special huge mushroom lived inside the jar, turning the water into a slightly bubbling nonalcoholic drink with a sweet and sour taste. I also liked *kvass*, which was sold on the street from a big cistern. Nobody worried about the cleanliness of the glasses in which *kvass* was served. I was never a fan of *kumis* because of its sour taste. *Kumis* is fermented mare's milk, and just the idea of drinking horse milk made my stomach turn.

The pears on our single but generous fruit tree ripened quickly, and I was never in time to taste their juicy sweetness. Overnight they turned from green and firm into nectar bombs, dropping to the ground and smashing into a pile of inedible juicy mash (*kasha*). Our wild apricot tree, called *uryuk*, produced hundreds and hundreds of *uryuchin*. They were like regular apricots but much smaller in size and not as tasty. It was impossible to collect even half of the fruit from the tall branches, and these little wild apricots found their destiny on the ground, easy food for the birds. There were a few lilac bushes, and a gorgeous jasmine bush with an amazingly refreshing smell. I loved watching the myriad of snails crawling along its branches, making their endless trips all day long.

One day my father bought me a turtle that I loved very much. This creature was always on the move, but as you can guess, it was quite slow. One day when I let it out to get some fresh grass from our yard, it crawled away, and I never found it. I hope someone found it and took good care of it. I also had an aquarium with guppies. I could watch them for hours; they were so beautiful, especially the male guppies. They had a big variety of colored spots and stripes to attract females (as I now know), and actually did quite well. From time to time I had to rescue newborn babies out of the aquarium since for some reason the parents liked to eat them right after birth! I put the babies in a separate jar and fed them until they got bigger. In a few weeks it would be safe to return them to the aquarium to be reconnected with their family. We always had a few chickens, which were kind enough to supply us with fresh eggs, but sometimes ended up in our soup. Our young German shepherd lived outdoors and always seemed angry. He did a good job protecting the house from possible invaders, but one time when our guests were leaving the house, he went totally crazy and broke his chain. I happened to be in his way and he bit me. Our guests escaped unharmed, but my father gave the dog away.

2 · Frunze

Frunze, formerly called Pishpek (Bishkek), was renamed in 1926 in honor of the Bolshevik revolutionary "liberator" Mikhail Frunze, who was born there. Mikhail Frunze was a close associate of Lenin's and played a key role during the revolutions of 1905 and 1917 as well as during the Russian civil war in the early 1920s. Frunze was and still remains the capital of and the largest city in Kyrgyzstan. Even though it was a suburb of the Russian empire, it had its own cultural life with concert halls, museums, and university. The Opera House was built in the classical tradition, and looked like it had been transplanted from Italy. There was a Philharmonic Hall, where I heard some very good guest artists, mostly violinists. The concerts were never sold out, but the audiences who came to the concerts were intelligent and dedicated.

One time we waited in the hall for a good hour for the artist to arrive. His plane had been delayed. Even though people did not know when he would arrive, no one left. It was getting late. When he finally arrived, he did not have time to change into concert attire, and played the entire program in his regular clothes, without an intermission. The other concert that left a strong impression on me starred Olga Parkhomenko. She was a former student of David Oistrakh and had been praised for her bright personality, great temperament, and unconventional musical interpretations. She played very well, but what impressed me and the rest of the audience was not only her good performance but also the funny facial expressions she made during the concert. This visual accompaniment was beyond description. It seemed that her face was made out of rubber, and I have never seen another face in my life with such flexible facial muscles. I laughed to tears through the entire concert and could not remember a note she played, but the price of the ticket had been well worth the cost.

Before I started collecting stamps, I collected match box stickers. The stickers had a rectangular shape and were quite colorful, featuring portraits of Russian cosmonauts, famous scientists, musicians, and heroes of WWII, as well as party leaders of the Socialist bloc. Some featured monuments, since every big Russian city had many squares with the inevitable distinguished poet, writer, or political leader cast proudly in bronze. On other stickers one might find the architectural wonders of the world, such as the Taj Mahal, Egyptian pyramids, or St. Petersburg's Hermitage. After all the matches were gone, I would unglue the stickers with water and wash them gently so the rest of the glue would melt away. Just before they completely dried out, I would put them between the pages of a heavy book to keep them flat. (I used the same heavy book technique to press collected leaves and flowers when I went to school and started studying botany.) I put those match box stickers in specially designed albums. It was an educationally interesting and valuable collection that cost me nothing: a box with matches cost one kopek (one cent) and would be thrown away after being emptied. It was as fascinating as any other collection could be, at least for me at the time. I would compare and trade match box stickers with other boys who had similar collections.

At the age of ten I became interested in photography, and my father bought me a nice camera, a "Zenith-3." It was a heavy, good quality camera in a thick leather case. That's how I became the designated family photographer. The camera used 36mm film, and it took me some time to learn how to load the film into the camera in total darkness, since the film was extremely sensitive to light. It was fun to take pictures of family members, flowers, trees, and animals, but I actually had far more fun developing the film from scratch. I loved making my own solutions and then sitting in the dark room with its red light manipulating the size, sharpness, and contrast of the image. There was no color photography available yet, and I still have quite a few black and white photographs from my childhood that I took myself. I think there is a certain expression in black and white photographs that color ones lack, very similar to old black and white movies.

Like most boys, I enjoyed sports. I played soccer and basketball with the neighbors (the hoop was attached to a poplar tree), and ping-pong on a homemade table. I was good at chess and even won a couple of games against my father. In wintertime there was skating at the ice rink. I even had my own skates! (You know why? We had to buy them because there was no rental service at that time.) My feet grew rapidly each year, and my parents had to buy me new skates almost every year.

One day I was taken to a soccer game featuring our local team, Dinamo. Before the gates were opened, a huge crowd collected in front of the stadium, excited and anxious to get the best seats. When the gates were finally opened, people pushed forward and I was lifted, finding myself pressed against a metal railing. I got stuck and in a fraction of a second realized that my ribs would be crushed. Then I heard my father scream, "Move to the side, twist!" For a brief moment, miraculously, the pressure lessened and I managed to slide my body to the side. That saved me. Otherwise, I would not be writing these lines today.

Frunze had a humid continental climate, full of contrasts. In winter the temperature could drop to minus 40 degrees Celsius (minus 40 Fahrenheit), sometimes snowing a couple of feet overnight. In such terrible cold the birds died instantly. They had to leave their warm nests to find food, and their frozen little bodies would lie in the snow till spring. Summers held steady at 35-40 degrees Celsius (around 100 Fahrenheit) or higher.

I have always believed that bad things could lead to good things, and when the temperature dropped below minus 25 Celsius (minus 13 Fahrenheit), the schools were closed. My mom would apply pig lard to my face to protect my skin from the frost, and let me out to have some fun and play with the neighbor kids. At this age we used to tease each other a lot with nasty words, and one time my words made the neighbor girl really angry. She threw a rock at me; I reacted quickly and turned my face away. The rock hit my head, and I started bleeding. It wasn't a big deal, but it could easily have taken out my eye. I never teased her again.

Summers were special: three months with no school speaks for itself. Frunze is a very green city, almost as green as Seattle. From the beginning of June all the grass would turn bright yellow, and there was not a drop of rain from the deep blue skies till at least October or so. Frunze had long, straight sidewalks for pedestrians with very tall poplars planted quite close to one another providing constant shade. When these trees started to bloom, suddenly it looked like winter. The fluffy white cotton balls went flying from the poplars for weeks, cloaking the city with clouds of feathery snow. The biggest fun came afterwards. The boys loved to throw a match into a pile of poplar seeds on the ground. A fire was lit and spread fast along the sidewalk, creating sparks and dying quickly. It was amazing to watch.

Frunze sits at the bottom of the Kyrgyz Ala-Too Mountains. The melting water from the mountains runs through *ariks*, supplying the city with vital moisture during the hot months. Like blood vessels in our body, *ariks* played a vital part in the irrigation system of Asian countries. They brought coolness to the air and life to the earth. The sides of the *ariks* were made of concrete with smooth rocks on the bottom. They were quite narrow, and my friends and I loved to sit in them and feel the gentle pressure of the water running around our bodies.

The very first time I experienced an earthquake was when I was five or six years old. I was outdoors and did not know how it should feel, but understood what it was instantly. The quake was mild and there was no damage done, but I did not like it at all. I have been afraid of them ever since. We did not have television, so I could not know what the worst earthquakes were capable of, but I later learned about the devastating earthquakes in neighboring republics when the beautiful cities of Ashkhabad and Tashkent were ruined in a matter of seconds.

The year 1962, when I was seven years old, was a terrifying year for people who lived in Kyrgyzstan. There was strong political tension between the Soviet Union and China based on a disagreement about territories, and these two giant countries were on the brink of war. At the time, Southern Kyrgyzstan shared a long border with China. There had already been a few serious military conflicts with China on the Far East part of the Russian border, but that was far from Kyrgyzstan. During the day Frunze looked like a normal city with its normal city life, but at night, countless lines of tanks and heavy artillery thundered down the streets to China's border. This went on for weeks.

Our house was on Sovietskaya Street, one of the major arterials in the city. At night the house trembled. We watched huge tanks from the window; the fumes and constant loud noise from the machines made sleep impossible. The tracks from those tanks stayed imprinted in the warm asphalt for years as a reminder that nothing is forever, especially peace. Soviet people still remembered the horrors of the past war, and everyone was unspeakably scared. It seemed that a bloody conflict was inevitable. Fears rose so high that many people fled the city to the North, away from the border, to find shelter with friends or relatives. We had nowhere to go, and our only hope lay in the uncrushable power of the Soviet military. There were rumors that the tank lines at the border were a kilometer wide!

Fortunately for millions and millions of people, the tension between the two countries gradually decreased, but it took almost a decade until relations between the USSR and China stabilized. We spent all those years living under the psychological pressure of the threat of war.

As a kid I often experienced colds and sore throats. My adenoids and tonsils became so swollen that I could hardly breathe. The doctor recommended removing them, since every cold would quickly become unbearable. I was maybe five years old, and did not know anything about what an operation meant. We arrived at the doctor's office, and I sat my brave little body in the chair. There was no anesthesia, and what followed was a nightmare. To remove my adenoids, the doctor made a loop with a thin metal wire (very similar to an "E" violin string), put it around the gland, tightened it, and pulled the string. It was no fun! My mouth got warm from the blood. The doctor put the second loop in my mouth, but the attempt to remove the second gland became complicated by the blood filling my mouth. The doctor could not see what he was doing, but still pulled the string. It was not successful, as only half of the gland got extracted. More blood pouring out of the wounds made further surgery impossible and I left the doctor's office with half a gland left and untouched tonsils. But the reward was amazing! I got an ice cream, because the cold was supposed to help stop the bleeding, though I did not get to choose the type of ice cream. They only had vanilla anyway, and it was good enough for me.

Perhaps I can blame my father's genes for this, but I always liked to express my physical strength by lifting heavy objects: big rocks, metal panels, anything. I even tried to lift my mother, but did not succeed. I did succeed in getting two hernias, one after the other. Two separate surgeries were performed, and after each I was not allowed to get up or move for a week. It was torture to lie on my back and especially to sleep on my back. On the seventh day when I was finally allowed to get up, the pain I experienced was the sharpest I have ever felt. It felt like a burning knife inside of me. My body healed nicely though, and I thought that the scars made me look manlier. Very soon I was climbing my favorite oak tree again, sitting on the branches, throwing acorns at my friends, and observing the world below.

As far back as I can remember, there was always music in our house. My sister practiced the piano all day long, mastering endless passages, and with time I knew all her pieces by memory. She was stubborn and hardworking, though I don't recall her ever being asked to play for guests. On special occasions my family would throw parties that would bring all our relatives who lived in the city together under one roof. There was always an abundance of food, drink, and a lot of singing. As soon as I was able to make a few sounds on my tiny violin, my father would show me off at these parties by asking me to play something, maybe just a few notes. None of the other kids in our extended family played violin. I had a good ear and could pick up almost any song. Later my "signature" pieces at parties were my father's favorite Brahms *Hungarian Dance No. 1*, which I performed in my slightly simplified version, and the melancholic *Polonaise* by Polish composer Michal Oginski.

Frunze had two artificial lakes with equally artificial names: Pioneer and Komsomolsk, with absolutely no connection to the Russian youth organizations bearing the same names.[1] We often went there on hot days. Since almost everybody wanted to cool down, and on any given summer there were half a million overheated inhabitants of Frunze, there was a problem getting to the lakes. We did not have a car, and to get there on bus route No. 4 presented a huge challenge. All the buses were packed to the roof, and we had to miss a few until a kind passenger would yell, "Comrades, squeeze in a bit, let a couple more people get on!" Once on the bus, the actual nightmare would begin. I was only half as tall as most people on the bus, and although I tried to lift my head, it

---

1 The Pioneer organization was comparable to the Boy Scouts in America. Komsomol was created for older kids who eventually would prepare to become members of the Communist Party.

always seemed to stick in somebody's stomach or butt. The stench of a few dozen sweaty bodies was unbearable. It felt like I was in an oven with 100% humidity, almost like in a Russian *banya*. But 45 minutes later, I would feel the sweet relief of the lake's cool water.

One time we went to the lake with my father for a swim. We left our clothes on the beach and upon returning discovered that some of our stuff was not there anymore, including my father's pants and watch. A man sitting at a distance pointed to three men walking away with our stuff. My dad rushed towards the men as they started to run. I ran after them but could hardly keep up. Eventually we entered a small park with no people around and the men stopped and turned as if they were expecting us. My father approached them and demanded the return of his pants and watch. One of the men took a knife out of his pocket with the obvious intention of threatening my dad, potentially even inflicting harm. I was standing behind my father, trying to catch my breath, not fully comprehending what was happening. My father stepped forward and said, "Do you think that after fighting the Nazis for four years I would be afraid of you?" A few seconds of terrible tension electrified the air. Then the man holding the knife said, "I am sorry, *pahan*. Don't be offended, we did not know that you were in the war." They handed over our things and retreated.

The word *pahan* is used in Russian prisons as a signal of respect. During the Soviet era, Stalin sent criminals away from major Russian cities to Asia, and the crime rate in Frunze was much higher than in Moscow or Leningrad. Sometimes we heard horrifying stories about brutal crimes around the city. My parents were scared, and I was scared too.

A highlight of my preschool years was our family trips to Lake Issyk-Kul. This is a natural lake surrounded by the Tian Shan Mountains about 180 kilometers from Frunze. The lake was often called 'The pearl of Asia' for its pure emerald water. It got its name, Issyk-Kul, which means 'hot lake' in the Kyrgyz language, because it never froze. It was a big privilege to get a *putevka* (a ticket) to get to a place referred to as a resort. If this "resort" were included in the Michelin 5 star ratings, it would have gotten zero stars. Since my father could not get a *putevka* for the whole family, he never went with us, but sent my mother, my sister, and me instead. The fun usually started with the transportation. We sat in an open truck on wooden benches and prepared for a five or six-hour trip. Sometimes the truck would break down, and we would wait with great patience for it to be fixed, which could take another few hours. My mother always packed a good amount of food for the trip and we would have a nice long picnic on such occasions. We got hungry quickly and often. Boiled eggs with a pinch of salt with each bite, a thick piece of rye bread, fresh, crunchy cucumbers, big juicy tomatoes, and of course cooked chicken – it was simple but tasty food. Looking around, most of the passengers had a similar assortment of "gourmet" food. Eventually the truck would be fixed and we would continue on our voyage. Most of the road traversed the mountains, and so one side of the road was always a sharp cliff. I was too terrified to look down.

We did not know how to protect ourselves from the burning sun. There was neither shade nor sun umbrellas, so after the first day we were all as red as the Russian flag. We applied kefir thickly all over our bodies to ease the pain of our severely burned skin. Three days later, all our skin would start coming off, leaving us looking like molting snakes, though I am sure snakes don't suffer as much as we did. This exposed the second layer of skin to be burned again, and a week later we returned home with ulcers all over our bodies. Our noses suffered the most, and it took at least a month for new skin to grow. But it was fun, in a Russian sort of way.

Typically, the weather on Lake Issyk-Kul during the summer was like that of Arizona: not a cloud in the sky, and very, very hot. One day I felt something strange in the air. The weather was somehow different. The sky had changed color from blue to grey and we could feel the wind pick up. Then I saw a huge waterspout in the middle of the lake. It looked like a gigantic whirlpool sucking water up into the grey skies, but luckily it was happening far away from the shore where we stood. We were safe.

3 · Central Market

One of Frunze's biggest attractions was the market. Most people didn't have cars, so we would all take the trolley or a bus. When we got off at the stop that led to the market, we didn't need to ask for directions. We could find it with our eyes closed. The bouquet of aromas, streaming in particular from the melons, covered at least a kilometer in radius. Especially impressive were the so-called Asian melons, slightly pink inside, which would sometimes reach almost two feet in length and weighed up to 50 pounds. The most remarkable aspect of this colossal fruit was its taste. When it was sliced open, the scent of the ripe fruit would pulse with energy through the air. Its variety of flavors can only be compared to the most exceptional red wines. We had to be careful eating it. Most of the fruit's juice would inevitably end up covering me up to my armpits.

To buy a melon, one had to go through a standard ritual. After a few minutes of knocking on the surface of at least a dozen beauties, my mother would stop the percussion test and point to the potential lucky choice. It had produced the most vibrancy in the lowest pitch compared with the others. I bet every customer at the market had perfect pitch when it came to melons! The vendor always praised his product, giving his guarantee of the quality of the melon. The next step was the tasting. The vendor, dressed rather warmly for the weather in a quilted robe with a felt hat on his head, would make a triangular incision in the melon and pull out a triangle with the end of his knife. "You see how red it is? Now taste it!" This was not a suggestion but rather an order. It's true that the taste was always delicious.

I loved grapes; the following two kinds were my favorites. "The Lady's Fingers" were gentle and green, long, juicy and sweet enough to be addicting. The other type was called "The Ox's Eye" and they were dark red, round, and huge in size with a tougher skin. Of course all grapes came with seeds in those days. I ate them not one by one, even though each grape was quite big for my little mouth, but stuffed in as many of them as I could. I loved to feel them being smashed all at once and feel that juicy sensation inside my cheeks. Many times my mother warned me that I would end up with appendicitis if the seeds got caught in my insides, but nothing could stop me from pursuing my pleasure.

Entering the market was like entering a whole new world. It was a unique kingdom with its own rules and history. If you ever decide to visit an Asian country in the summertime and find yourself at a market, my first recommendation is to get some sunblock. Second, skip the dark glasses. Vendors need to see your eyes, especially when you begin to bargain, an inevitable process of purchasing something at the market. In the end, the process of bargaining isn't really about the money, but rather about the fun. At a market, one doesn't talk gossip or politics, which tend to be acceptable and popular topics in any other setting. At the market, you'd better save your conversational energy for bargaining. This market was the source of all our groceries during the spring and summer.

At the time, local grocery stores impressed neither foreigners nor locals. The variety of products was extremely poor. One could buy cheese. There were only two types of cheese: Rossiyskiy and Dutch. Except for a slight difference in price, there wasn't a detectable difference in flavor between the two. To get white bread my father would wake up at 6:00 in the morning and rush to the bakery only to find that he was not the first in line. When the bakery opened at 7:00, there would be a limited supply of white bread (but plenty of dark rye bread), so only the first 10-15 lucky customers would be able to bring this luxury home for breakfast to spoil their kids a bit.

Fish, however, was plentiful. I remember a large fish tank across the street from which one could scoop carp or *som* (a kind of catfish) to one's heart's content and have dinner prepared within 15 minutes. Sometimes my parents would buy a big fish, bring it home, and place it, still alive, into a bowl of water where it would swim for several hours until its time came. My mother made phenomenal gefilte fish. It was her signature savory dish. I have not yet mustered the courage to make my own.

My mother was an exceptional cook, as was my sister. As far as I remember, my dad and the other men in our extended family did not cook. I suppose that made me the first to express an interest in the craft and, according to my kids and friends, I haven't done too badly. My mother often experimented with new recipes, and one day someone told her she could have fresh tomatoes year-round. The instructions were very simple: cover the bottom of a glass jar with a thin layer of dry mustard, add a few fresh whole tomatoes, and seal the jar. These jars would then be stored in a dark closet and opened as needed, usually in the wintertime, when finding fresh produce was out of the question.

Approximately one week after my mother had finished preserving a large amount of tomatoes, we were awakened from our sleep once or twice by strange noises. They seemed to be coming from outside the house. We didn't pay them much attention for the first couple of nights, but then it really started to bother us, especially due to the fact that Frunze was not the safest of cities. As we heard the sound on the third night, my dad woke up, took in hand a large piece of wood, and ventured toward the front door. When he examined the area around the house, he noticed nothing out of the ordinary. He came back inside, declaring everything safe, and the sound came again, frightening us out of our wits. It was obviously coming from the closet where we kept the tomatoes. My father opened the closet door and was amazed by the gory mess. A thick red paste covered the walls and floor. The dry mustard powder combined with the fresh tomatoes had chemically reacted to release a gas. The pressure inside the jars had become so intense that the lid was forced off in a powerful explosion. Unfortunately for us, with the particularly tightly sealed jars, the gas had found its way out by erupting through the bottoms of the jars. The only challenge now was to carefully open the remaining intact jars, which we did. No one got hurt. As far as I remember, this was my mother's only unsuccessful culinary endeavor.

Her borscht was unsurpassable and just thinking about her sour cherry piroshky makes my mouth water. Finding something close to that sweet and sour taste has been an obsession for me all these years, but I have never succeeded in finding anything that comes close to my mother's masterpiece.

4 · My Parents

My father was born in the small town of Szibulev, close to Uman, not far from Kiev. His Jewish name was Pinya, and he was physically a very strong man. When he was young he could walk on his hands back and forth across the yard many times. At that time, he worked at the cow slaughterhouse, and it was common practice for the people who worked there (my father included) to drink steaming cow's blood right on the spot. They said it made them strong. My father was an idealist and a patriot, committed to the idea of building a new fair society. He taught history as a profession. Like millions of other Russian citizens, he had been arrested without explanation during Stalin's time and tortured.

He was a very organized person and had a great memory for dates. He prepared his daily lectures the night before, even though he already knew the material by heart. He had very "sophisticated" hand writing, and quite often could not read what he had written down minutes before. Often he would ask my mother to do the writing for him. Energetically pacing from one corner of the room to the other, he dictated his lectures with emotion and conviction, and it was clear that people would listen to his words. He was a born leader. Every lesson was like a one-man show. Students loved him and referred to him as an artist of his trade.

He was a devoted father, and tried to spend as much time with me as possible. When I was still a small child, he arranged a long tour with me to the place where he was born. Unfortunately, I don't remember anything except for three long days on the train just to get to Moscow, and then changing trains to reach Ukraine. The trains were stuffy and tiring, and I was glad to be back home. Sometimes my dad took me to the shooting range. I loved shooting with my left eye closed, aiming at the black circle. The light bullet would fly like a bee toward the circle and pop the paper, making a tiny hole in the target. Every time I managed to make a hole in the dark circle, my father beamed with pride.

As I grew, I ate a lot and I ate often. Sometimes late at night I would complain to my dad that I was hungry. He would jump out of bed and bring me the most delicious sandwich I could imagine at that time: dark bread sprinkled with sunflower seed oil and salt.

He is the one responsible for my becoming an organized person, and he taught me to make a list of "what to do tomorrow" every night before going to bed. I still do it.

My father literally saw the world in black and white, as he was color blind. He had a choleric temperament, was explosive, and easily carried away, often carrying others with him. I could tell he was not an easy man to live with. One of his dreams was to buy a car. We saved money on everything, and each day that passed brought us a little closer to our goal. But one day when my father opened his newspaper, *Pravda* ("Truth"), he found that the prices for cars had doubled overnight without explanation. His dream was like a Soviet mirage, the closer he came to it, the farther it moved away. This did not entirely sink his dream, but likely planted a seed of doubt in his faith in the system. I wondered who would drive the car even if we were able to buy it one day.

Father was a fighter for the truth. He would never accept half measures, conformism, or weakness in people. His color blindness transferred onto his relationships with others. It was either right or wrong, never in-between. At some point he quarreled with his brother and did not forgive him to his last day. This meant that we cut off relations with the closest family we had. He was often sick; his heart gave him a lot of trouble, but he made it to age 84. In 1990, my father, mother, sister, and her husband immigrated to Israel. At that time there was no way for them to join me in America. He was 78 when their plane landed in Tel Aviv, and he never learned a phrase of Hebrew.

My mom was a kind and calm person, always a peacemaker, trying to smooth the sharp edges of her husband's character. She was a protector of her children, often from the anger of our father. She was two years younger than my father, and lived till she was nearly 91. She was also a dream interpreter for our family. Our family was superstitious, like many families back then. Every morning we would tell her our dreams, and she would find meaning in them. We were mesmerized by the mystic life beyond the physical world. Anxiously we listened to how those dreams would affect our lives. And you know, very often she was right. For example, if we lost a tooth in our dream, it meant that we would hear the next day that somebody had died. In those days, funeral processions slowly moving down the streets were common. This was all the proof we needed that our dreams were coming true! If the dreamt tooth fell out with the presence of blood, this meant that a relative would die. We were always relieved when no bad news had come by the end of the day.

Do you remember an exciting dream when you were flying, feeling the incomparable sensation of the weightlessness of your body? The magic of that state meant that we were growing. Adults seldom have such amazing dreams. After graduating from college my main nightmare was that I had to play a piano exam (piano was our secondary instrument at the college) and I could not remember the notes. My left and right hands did not want to cooperate, and a terrible cacophony emerged from the piano. Later when I started my professional career as an orchestra violinist, the nightmares shifted to "the misplaced violin" ("Damn it, I swear I remember I'd put it right there!"), or not being properly dressed for a concert ("Why I am still in jeans and where is my bow tie?"), while the orchestra was already on stage tuning up. In such dreams, the concert halls, countries, and people are all mixed up. I still have those dreams. I wonder what a psychologist would make of them.

I learned the secrets of dream interpretation from my mother firsthand, and practiced it often with my children. Now I am trying to let go of superstitions in my life, ignoring my dreams and trying to forget them as soon as I wake up. I want to feel more in charge of my life and not depend on something beyond my control. But when I see a black cat crossing the road in front of me, I never cross the cat's path. I dream every night, but rarely see my parents in my dreams, which seems strange.

We never celebrated Jewish holidays in our family. We did not know (or at least I didn't) where they fell on the calendar, and we never attended synagogue. It was prohibited for Jews to practice their religion and every person who attended synagogue was placed on "the list." As principal of a school, my father could not afford that, as it would result in immediate termination of his job. At home, my parents often spoke Yiddish, but just so that the children would not understand "adult" talk. Since my childhood I have known that I was a Jew, but I had no idea what it really meant, except maybe that Jews were talented musicians, and not very loved by other people. Later, after arriving in America where I have had many opportunities to explore my heritage, I never felt that I was a Jew. The religion itself is of interest to me only from a historical perspective. Maybe we intuitively tried to escape our past fears by rejecting our DNA on a subconscious level. Now I rather feel myself a citizen of the world, or just a man without a nationality, slowly growing into the feeling of becoming American.

5 · UFO

We had recently moved into a new two-bedroom apartment in a five-story building without an elevator. We did, however, get central heating, running water, and a toilet in the apartment. The flat was on the third floor and my room overlooked the mountains. It was one of those hot and stuffy summer nights, and a deep darkness came upon the city. It was very quiet but I could not fall asleep. The air was clear, the moon high in the skies, and from my bed I could see the silhouette of the mountains. Everything was unbelievably calm; not a leaf stirred. This calmness was typical for summer nights. I continued reading my book for a while, and eventually my eyelids became heavy. It was way after midnight, and I fell asleep.

Suddenly I awoke. My first sensation was that I was in a whirlpool. There was a terrible wind and the open windows were rattling like crazy. I jumped off the bed to close them, afraid they might break. There was a dust storm and I could not see a thing. With the windows closed it instantly became very stuffy and impossible to sleep. In a few minutes the wind stopped like somebody had suddenly turned off a switch, and the dust settled. I opened my windows again and looked at the mountains. What I saw was something unusual and I grew very curious. There were three lights. First I thought it was a fire on the slope of the mountains, which would be a common sight in summertime, but the lights did not move at all and there was no smoke. Then I realized that the lights were suspended way above the mountains. There was something very exciting about it. The lights were definitely neither helicopters nor military planes. Since the distance between my bedroom and the lights was at least a few kilometers, that type of machinery could not possibly have created such a storm. I had read about natural phenomena but could not find a better explanation for what I was witnessing than it being an extraterrestrial event.

I rushed to my parents' bedroom, woke them up, and dragged them into my room. They were amazed. We continued to stare at the lights for a while, and whatever they were, they did not move at all. Soon we grew too tired and went back to bed. Some time later I was awakened for the second time by the loud rattling of my windows. Dust was again flying into my room. Already suspecting something, I jumped up to look out the window. The wind was calming down and the dust started to settle. I looked at the mountains: there were no more lights. I recognized the familiar skyline of the mountains. The moon was peacefully shining from above, not surprised at all by the activity below.

I don't have any doubts that what I witnessed was a UFO. I did not discuss this with other people, and there was nothing about it in the newspapers, not the next day, not ever. This kind of information was always kept secret in Russia.

Almost 50 years later I met a woman in Seattle who shared with me a story very similar to my own. It was in 1975 in Moscow and she and her friend were on the underground train on their way home from work. They got off at their station, Belyaevo. It was one of the newer neighborhoods of Moscow, approximately fifty minutes by train from the city's center.

While leaving the station they noticed a crowd outside, probably commuters from the previous train, transfixed and staring up at the sky. A large object, round and all lit up, was suspended in the air. It wasn't an airplane, she said, as it wasn't moving, and hung there in complete silence.

It was around 5:00 in the evening and dusk was settling onto the city. Soon it grew dark, but the illuminated object was still hanging in the air. As the evening darkened, its lights seemed to grow brighter and brighter in contrast with the changing sky. Approximately half an hour passed with no change. The people were starting to get cold and, shivering in the November air, they dispersed and headed to their respective homes.

There was no mention of the event in the media. It isn't hard to imagine the kind of panic such news could have ignited among the Muscovites. I don't have any reason to disbelieve this woman's story. The friend who was with her that evening now lives in Chicago and also clearly remembers the episode. They claim that what they saw, without a doubt, was a flying saucer. This was proof enough to me that we are not alone in the cosmos.

6 · Music School

My father was totally tone deaf, but always tried to hum his favorite folk songs. It was my mother from whom I inherited perfect pitch. Classical music was in big favor at that time in Russia. The names of David Oistrakh, Sviatoslav Richter, and Mstislav Rostropovich were on the front pages of newspapers and on the radio. These outstanding musicians were national heroes, idols, the image of a great society and a good life. No wonder my parents tried to give a better future to their children by providing them with a musical education.

That is exactly what happened when I turned seven. All children in the USSR went to school at the age of seven. This applied to music school as well. There was no question in our family that I would learn music. The question was: which instrument? Before that could be decided, I had to pass a test that consisted of three sections: repeating rhythm patterns, singing a melody, and recognizing pitch. The last one was the trickiest. The examiner asked me to turn away so I could not see the keys of the piano (it really did not matter, since they all looked the same to me anyway). He would play a key, and then I would have to find the same key by poking around for it. He did it three times, and each time I found the right key. He was impressed, and later I understood why. I was blessed to have "perfect" pitch, a rare quality that means that I can identify any pitch I hear. (As an adult, I have had fun impressing my colleagues by identifying the pitch of flying airplanes or the sounds of a braking car, calling it out as an F-sharp or B-flat, for example.) I was accepted to the school right away. Since we already had a pianist in the family, my parents followed the suggestion of the man who tested me and signed me up for the violin.

I remember well the glorious day when I proudly carried my tiny violin in its tiny violin case that I was not allowed to open ("the violin is a very fragile," I was told) to my first lesson. I was very excited and could not wait. Especially valuable to me had been the book *Condemnation of Paganini* by Russian writer Anatoly Vinogradov. My father had given it to me as a gift, even though I could not yet read. Later, this little work of fiction that was full of mysterious and compelling stories about the world's greatest violin virtuoso would become my favorite, and I reread it a dozen times till it fell apart.

My introduction to the violin went smoothly. I loved my violin teacher and she loved me. She became like a mother to me. One time my father came to pick me up after my lesson. It was well past the end time. He waited and then knocked at the door and asked permission to take me home. My teacher apologized for taking more time than usual and said that I could go home. According to my father, I grabbed the teacher around the waist with all the passion I was capable of and yelled that I was not going home and wanted to practice more. The story became a family legend.

I don't recall ever being forced to practice the violin. By the second grade I was practicing up to five hours a day, mostly while looking out the window. I memorized my music quickly and mechanically repeated it while daydreaming. And of course there was public school every day, but homework was very easy. I always completed my homework very quickly and managed straight A's.

My progress at music school did not go unnoticed, but this was where my problems started. The principal of the music school was also a violin teacher, and he decided he wanted me in his class. Some dirty politics were involved, which neither I nor my parents were aware of, and at the beginning of the sixth grade I was moved to a different teacher. By the end of the school year my grades had gone down and my violin playing had fallen off as well. The new teacher and I had absolutely no chemistry. I got a C-minus on the violin exam. I needed to be saved. The savior, the principal of the school, took me back into his class with the hope that I could recover my skills. It worked, and within a few months I became a star of the school: concertmaster of and a soloist in the school orchestra, even performing as a soloist on TV playing *Siciliana and Rigaudon* by Fritz Kreisler.

In those days I played on a violin that was not handmade, but made in a factory. Later we would joke that it was made in a furniture factory. This might have been true; it looked like it was made from yellow veneer, the same wood from which cheap dressers are made, and it had a very primitive, one-dimensional sound quality. Since my career was on the rise, the teacher told my father that I needed a better violin. My father loved me and wished me the best, but he had absolutely no knowledge of violins. I suspect that he thought there was only one type of violin, the one I already had in my hands. When the teacher said that he had a violin in mind, and it would cost one hundred rubles (half of my dad's monthly salary), my father went ballistic. Public education was free in the USSR, except for music. The fee for studying at the music school was seven rubles a month. It took my dad some time to adjust to the idea that music education might cost some money on top of what we already paid.

Finally, he scraped to-gether 100 rubles from the family savings, and I be-came the proud owner of an old German violin made at a German factory. It was a beautiful fiddle and had much better sound. One day, while walking down the stairs after my lesson, my violin case suddenly opened up (I had forgot-ten to lock it), the violin fell on the granite steps, and rolled down half a flight. I almost lost my mind. I was so scared that I had ruined it. I picked it up only to see that nothing was broken, there was not even a scratch, and it was

Age 11

not even out of tune! I never told this story to my parents.

My father bought me my first records and a record player. Those recordings not only became my favorites, but my obsession. The be-ginning of the first movement of Mozart's Symphony No. 40 in G Minor with Toscanini conducting will haunt me all my life. Jascha Heifetz performing Khachaturian's *Saber Dance* made him an idol to me (and to millions of music lovers around the world). Mischa

Elman playing Schubert's *Ave Maria* had a hypnotizing sound on his violin. I have never heard such deep and rich tones on any violin since. Thirty years later I actually played a concert with the Seattle Symphony Orchestra with a young soloist who performed his concerto on the violin that had earlier belonged to Misha Elman. I did not hear the magnetizing sound I had heard on Elman's recording. It was gone. This reminds me of a wonderful story: after a concert, an excited lady approached world-famous virtuoso Jascha Heifetz and told him that his violin sounded amazing. The great violinist brought his Guarneri to his ear and said, "I don't hear anything!"

By the time I was 12, I had attended three different public schools. In the first one there were 34 students in class. Three of them were hooligans and always fought. Three were straight-A students. (I bet you can guess which group I belonged to.) I had a good friend in the class, Alesha Salnikov. We lived near each other, were good students, and liked to spend time together. This caused jealousy in those hooligans and they managed to break our friendship apart. They turned my friend so much against me that one day the tension between us came to a breaking point. My friend said that he wanted to fight me. The white glove, as we used to say, was thrown on the ground in front of me.

I was never a troublemaker, nor a fighter. I did not know how to fight, but I had no choice but to accept the challenge. After the last lesson of the day, we went to the school yard where all those hooligans and other interested parties collected to see the fight till first blood between these A students and former friends. It was quite a rare occasion. My friend rushed toward me first, waving his fists, and I felt some strange power push me toward him. I don't recollect exactly what happened, but I did not feel any pain from his kicks, just a pulsation in my head. I must have hit him because I heard a scream, and saw the blood on his face. He surrendered, the fight stopped, and I started to cry. I cried because of our broken friendship, and that I had caused pain to my best friend. At that moment the world changed for me. I realized that it was not a simple place and that dark jealousy could easily destroy fragile human relationships. That was a painful lesson.

Soon I left that school because my parents wanted me to have more educational challenges. I joined a new school with an accelerated program in English. To catch up with the program, my parents hired a tutor, and during the summer I took ten intense private English lessons, studying language at home up to ten hours a day. I liked it very much, and soon became the best student in English class. We also had English lessons in geography, literature, and history, and soon I started to dream exclusively in English.

When I was in the seventh grade, my final year at the music school, I was told that a famous violin teacher, Julia Breitburg from Moscow, was coming to Frunze to hear the local talent. If she found them good enough, she would pick some students to be admitted to her class in Moscow. This was my lucky break. She liked me, but I had not yet turned thirteen, and my mother could not imagine letting me go to that huge and scary city of almost ten million people to live there alone. She cried all the time. To her, I was still a baby. In many ways she was right.

After I was chosen to go to Moscow, I had to be accepted into the ninth grade at the special music school, named after its founder Mikhail Gnessin. Up to this point, I had been enrolled in the same grade level at both public and music school through the seventh grade. It was decided that I would be allowed to skip eighth grade in music, but I had to get a formal paper showing I had finished eight years of public school education. I transferred into an evening school for working people just to get the formal paper. It was strange to share the same desk with students who were 10 to 30 years older than me, but it worked. Plus, everybody in the class liked me because I always helped them with projects.

Summers were the best time. I have to admit that I never touched my violin during those three months of vacation. I guess my hands had good muscle memory; after a few hours of practicing I could return to my pre-vacation shape. Often I was bored; there was not much to do for an introverted kid like me. Movies were great. Ten kopeks (about 10 cents) for a 10:00 a.m. movie was a good deal, and after that I could afford to have a glass of sweet sparkling water for three kopeks, or even an ice cream for nine kopecks, and spend my last four kopeks on the trolley to get home.

My experience riding a bike did not take me far. A friend once gave me a bike and explained how to ride it. I was fine for the first few meters, but then the road went a bit downhill, and I got scared

when I saw a huge hole in front of me. There was construction going on for a new apartment building, and the hole was at least two
meters deep. I tried to move away from it, but the more I tried the
more my bike kept moving toward the hole. I remember falling in.
I flipped in the air and fell, landing on my stomach, and my bike
hit me a moment later in the middle of my back. The panic was terrible, because I could not breathe at all. It was probably just a few
seconds, but my lungs were paralyzed. Finally, I was able to take a
short breath, and instantly felt a sharp pain in my back. The bike's
handle bar bent when it hit my back. I was lying on the ground unable to get up. My friend was next to me, scared, because my face
was bluish, my eyes were closed and I did not respond to his voice.
Then I slowly got up, leaving the bike behind, and went home. I did
not say anything to my parents, lay down in bed, and fell asleep. I
was sore for a few days, but was lucky that I didn't break any ribs. I
forgot about the incident quickly, but since then have never been a
good biker. I jog instead.

My parents made one attempt to send me to the local Pioneer
Camp, but I hated all the stupid songs we had to sing and the whole
Boy Scout atmosphere. I was maybe ten years old, and did not fit
into the group at all. I cried all the time, and soon my father had to
rescue me. But another attempt to introduce me to social life was
more successful. As a straight-A student, I was chosen to join other
top students from all over the Soviet Union at the Pioneer Camp
Artek in Crimea. This camp was of the highest quality; it was part
of the socialist propaganda machine. We even had to wear certain
uniforms which were provided for us for free as part of the package. Even the airfare was covered by the government. I liked that
camp because I fell in love there for the first time in my life. Marina
was about my age, a gorgeous brunette with a short haircut and
lovely dark skin. Her eyes were like two black olives, and she never
learned that I was crazy in love with her.

7 · *Moscow*

In 1969, Moscow was twenty times bigger in population than Frunze. Upon arrival I found that my future teacher had already reserved a place for me to stay. For the next three years I would live in a communal flat with an 82-year-old woman, sharing her nine square meter room. Technically I rented a corner of her room. My corner included a small bed. That was it. Her bed was separated from my corner by a screen (*shirma*). There were five other inhabitants in the four-bedroom apartment. The seven of us shared one bathroom, one telephone, and a kitchen with four cooking tables, each reflecting the character of its owner. Once a week I would call my parents and mom always asked, "Mishenka, do you miss us?" I have to admit there was not a single day I missed Frunze or my family. It was not because I did not love my parents, but because my life had become so filled with new experiences that there was no room for nostalgia. Moving to Moscow was my first immigration, and I did not look back.

Before I tell you about my landlady, let me briefly describe the other inhabitants of our apartment. The room next to the one I lived in was occupied by a woman in her seventies, who was totally deaf. One would expect a deaf person to talk loudly since they cannot hear themselves, but that woman was very quiet. Like a ghost she moved through the darkness of the corridor. (We tried to save energy since we all shared the bill for the shared spaces and rarely turned on the lights. The street light barely made it to the corridor.) She never looked at anybody and I don't remember her ever saying "hi" to the neighbors. She was a mystery to all of us.

The couple that lived in the next room was noisy. He was recently retired; his wife was at least 10 years younger and still worked. She was nearsighted and wore glasses with very thick lenses. She could only see a foot in front of her, and when I looked in her eyes they had a very funny shape, abnormally round. These two fought constantly about everything. They did not have kids, and probably were just tired of each other. The fourth room was occupied by a tiny lady with a hunchback. Szhenia had bad lungs. She was a kind person of uncertain age who did not work and also rented a corner of her room to another violinist, with whom I became friends.

This young fellow who was studying at a different school absolutely could not control his spending. He was always short of money, having nothing at all in his pockets (except for holes) and sometimes had to eat starch melted in sweet water. From time to time Szhenia would take pity on him and share with him her modest rations.

I do not recall anybody at our apartment having visitors. The six-story house we lived in was built from brick, as most houses were located in downtown Moscow. Our house was solid and all of the apartments had high ceilings. It had a noisy elevator that I could hear in the middle of the night, but it rarely disturbed my sleep. I slept well in those days.

My landlady and roommate (her name was Sophia, but people nicknamed her Sophochka because they liked her) rarely cooked, and I had my meals at the school's student cafeteria. A three-course meal cost 27 kopeks, or about 30 cents. A few years later, when I was a college student living in a dormitory, I would call Sophochka once a week just to check on her. Sometimes I would visit her. One time I called her and she said, "Mishenka, I was expecting you to come yesterday. I made two cutlets for us, but you did not come and I gave away your cutlet to the doggy." I bet that doggy was very happy.

Sophochka was a tiny woman with artistic genes. Her late husband, a musician, did not leave her a fortune, so she tried to make a little money by renting a part of her room to students. I was not her first student renter. My two predecessors had made good careers in music, and the outlook for me from that point was very positive. The age difference between us was almost 70 years, and I had just entered puberty. My teenage habits clashed with the habits of an old single woman, producing a lot of tension between us. We argued most about putting things back in their proper place, since she had her own system established at least 50 years before I arrived! From time to time we would have to sign a peace agreement.

By strange coincidence, my new place was located on Frunze Street. The spirit of Mikhail Frunze on his horse, dragging the *basmachei* (the bad guys) out of Asia followed me all the way to Moscow! The apartment I lived in was on the ground floor of a multistory building. The Russian Ministry of Defense had its headquarters right next door. Despite the heavy presence of armed soldiers, it did not make people who lived in the neighborhood feel any safer.

It was a nice October Sunday afternoon in 1970. The school and its cafeteria were closed on Sundays. Traditionally on that day I would go to the famous Café Praga to have a treat. There was always a big line of people who wanted to get a sausage or a cutlet with sour cabbage as a side dish. Normally it would take more than an hour to get the food, but I was not in a hurry. There was so much to discuss with the person next to me in line, a total stranger, who unexpectedly would become my best buddy. The most delicious dish was an appetizer, the only one on the menu. It was a hardboiled egg, sliced in half, with one half gracefully laying on the other. There was something almost erotic about it. Tasty mayonnaise was generously poured over the egg. By the time we got to the food line, the mayonnaise had developed a distinguished Mediterranean suntan.

I was on my way to the Café Praga when three guys much taller and stronger than me approached me and formed a triangle. One guy stood in front with his two henchmen behind, like in a crime movie. They were nice and simply asked for money. There was no need to threaten me with a knife, which I knew was in their pockets, or beat such a nice Jewish boy as me in front of the Ministry of Defense. I was scared and gave them what they asked for. It was just one ruble, the cost of my lunch at the Café Praga.

Just across from the apartment where I lived was a small food store where we usually bought groceries. The delivery truck came in the morning, and everybody knew it by the delicious smell coming from the freshly baked white bread. The aroma would be carried in the air, getting into every apartment and every little corner, and people would rush to get in line. A few steps led down to the store's underground level, the source of the intoxicating smell. Happy customers would buy a still warm baguette (what a luxury! I never tasted that kind of bread in Frunze). It was the addictive sweet aroma that made people happy. I have never experienced such addiction to fresh bread since. There was also bologna called *Doctorskaya* (Doctor's), a bit pink and also very tasty. The baguette and bologna went very well together, not very sophisticated, but it was delicious, and you would not dream of anything else after that gourmet sandwich.

In the 1970s, Russia had a very simple monetary system: no checks or credit cards. Everybody had cash in their pockets. It made it easier for muggers as well as everybody else. The whole salary system was primitive. People were paid once a month in cash. Basic taxes were taken out on the spot, and there was no 50-page tax return due by April 15th. The biggest problem was that many men would spend literally all their money on vodka right away, and then their wives had to scrape together money from friends till next payday. Very often women would wait at the office on pay day to get the money from their men, leaving them a few rubles for vodka. Saint Payday had to be celebrated. Viva Russia!

During the three years of my study at the Gnessin Moscow Special School of Music (we called it "*Gnessinka*"), twice a year I would get on a plane to visit my parents. At that time Russian airplanes did not have good sound insulation. Four powerful engines with big propellers built in front of the wings made a tremendous noise, and after a six-hour flight the roaring sound would stay in my ears for days. Fortunately, it did not affect my perfect pitch.

Political discussions were standard in every family and still remain so. It's no wonder that my visits always created tension between my father and me. We were all deeply influenced by Soviet propaganda when making comparisons between the two societies, Capitalists and Socialists. It was the Cold War, and the socialist society, according to the Soviet media, was always winning over heartless capitalism, though some people grew to have a different opinion on that matter. I would meet such people ten years later.

When I was about 15 years old, I expressed an interest in women's fashion. The reason was that my sister was in dating mode and wanted to have better clothing than anything the local department store could offer. The variety of women's clothes was not that limited, but it was of very poor quality and lacked imagination. That's when my deeply latent talent woke up. I decided to design a nice modern summer version of a Russian *sarafan* dress for my sister. I had never done anything like it and I was excited about the project. The idea came instantly into my mind. It was simple, and I started from scratch. I drew some variations on paper and let my sister choose which she liked the most. Then we bought fabric, I cut out the parts, and my sister sewed them together. Here is a picture of my sister in that "revolutionary" creation:

Before leaving Frunze for another half year of studying, my fa-

My sister Larisa in the sarafan that I designed

ther always gave me a stack of cash so I could pay my rent (25 rubles a month for my corner), buy food, and pay for other necessary expenses. I think he was quite impressed to see me return home six months later with some unspent cash to return to him. I proved to him that I could be responsible even at my young age.

8 · The Mausoleum

Since the 14th century, Moscow had been the capital of Russia. After a two-century gap during which its capital status was relinquished to St. Petersburg, it once again reclaimed its title following the Bolshevik Revolution, this time as the capital of the Soviet Union. The Kremlin, the heart of the Russian capital, has always been considered the most sacred place in Russia. For centuries, Mother Russia's fate was decided behind its walls. The Kremlin stands in Red Square (*Krasnaya Ploshchad*), which was paved in 1804 and is historically imprinted with the boot marks of thousands upon thousands of soldiers marching in military parades and the tracks of tanks carrying the Red Army's giant missiles. Red Square is actually not red in color; in Russian, the word *krasnaya* means both "red" and "beautiful."

Vladimir Ulyanov, Russia's first leader, is historically better known by his pseudonym: Lenin. It was common for Russian revolutionaries to take pseudonyms, but historians still cannot agree on the meaning behind his chosen name. Lenin died in 1924 and a mausoleum was erected in the center of Red Square in his honor. Russia's next communist leader, Josef Jughashvili, took the pseudonym Stalin, which comes from the Russian word *stal*, meaning "steel." True to his name, he ruled the country for nearly 30 years. Russians credited Stalin for winning World War II, and when he died in 1953 the whole country was deeply bereaved. Stalin's tremendous popularity made him a qualified candidate for the mausoleum. Lenin had to move a bit and share his place with the new "tenant." Stalin rested in his burial chamber until eight years later when Russians learned that their "Father of the Nation" was more of a monster than a saint. Documents that had come to light showed the Russian people (as well as the rest of the world) the horrible atrocities Stalin had committed against his own people: almost 30 million Russian people died in Gulags (Soviet forced labor camps) on his orders. After eight years of occupying the mausoleum, Stalin's waxed body was removed and reburied in the Kremlin Wall, a place reserved for party leaders of less importance.

To visit Lenin in the mausoleum was a sort of pilgrimage for

Russian people. On the day of my visit I had to be in line no later than five in the morning. The line was already huge, and the doors didn't open until ten. At 1:00 p.m. the doors of the mausoleum would be closed until the following visiting day. The line was very slow moving; a group of KGB officers stood at evenly spaced intervals and controlled the pace. People did not chit chat while they waited. Upon entering the mausoleum itself, men removed their hats as a sign of respect for the dead. No photography was allowed.

A thick pane of bulletproof glass protected the sarcophagus, and the transition from daylight to the dimly lit room required some time for the eyes to adjust. I could barely make out the pale figure inside. I was not impressed.

The whole experience left me with the feeling that it was all some sort of setup, that the mummy lying motionless in his grave was actually a hired actor. He'd wait until the final visitors had been ushered out, and when the doors closed at 1:00 pm, he would move the glass panel to the side, get up, and stretch his stiffened arms and legs. I imagined it to be a farce, an attempt to fool Russian people into thinking this once-powerful leader, the god of communism, still held some sort of power over them. My head swirling with surreal thoughts, I slowly made my way out of the dark and stuffy room. Back outside in the fresh air and sunshine, I felt a sense of relief.

9 · Gnessin Special School of Music

At Gnessin School I was the only student who did not actually live in Moscow. (Today the Gnessin School of Music accepts the most talented pupils from all over Russia and has built its own seven-story dormitory.) Moscow, the great capital of the USSR, strictly controlled its population. One couldn't just come to the city and stay there unless they were visiting relatives or coming as a tourist. One had to receive permission to stay in Moscow, and this could only happen for work or study related reasons. A special stamp called a *propiska* could be found in everybody's passport. This stamp would show at which address the person lived. At the end of the study term, the student was required to go back to his place of *propiska*.

Since I could not practice violin in my corner at home, I did it at school, usually in the evenings when classes were over and the rooms were empty. The school would be closed, but all the security guards knew me and would gladly open the door to any classroom. The weekends were the best. I had a choice of any room because the school was totally empty. My favorite was a big classroom with an old comfortable armchair. On class days the teacher sat in that chair all day long giving advice to youngsters on how to become the next Oistrakh or Richter. On Sundays I was the king. My day would start with a long nap in that famous chair. Nothing disturbed the total silence of the empty school. Upon waking, I felt hungry. I was thirteen and hungry all the time.

One day I was blessed with a delicious *olive* or "Russian salad" as it is known in America. One of the security guards invited me to a feast the likes of which I'd never had in my student years. Evidently there had been a party the day before, and generous leftovers had been saved in the cafeteria fridge. A large bucket was filled to the brim with the delicious salad. We grabbed big spoons and dug into the mushy mass. For a while not a word was said, and the only sounds were of clanking spoons and chewing. As one can guess, a long nap followed. Nothing could compare to that feast, not even Café Praga.

One Sunday I came to school to discover that my favorite

practice room was taken. I heard the sounds of a violin coming through the double doors and I grew quite curious. Who else would be practicing at school on a Sunday? I recognized the piece. It was *Perpetual Motion* by Niccoló Paganini, but it was being played at a suspiciously slow tempo. Though usually mechanical sounding, this piece transformed into an attractive virtuoso miniature when played at a very fast tempo. My curiosity forced me to open the first door and I listened to the mystery musician play the piece slower than I'd ever heard it played. After a few minutes my curiosity got the best of me, and I gently creaked open the second door. There stood Boris Garlitsky, one of the older students in our school and the son of famous violin teacher Mikhail Garlitsky, who also taught at the Gnessin School.

Boris stopped playing to greet me. I apologized for the interruption and asked what had brought him to practice at school on a Sunday. He said that his dad was preparing students for a recital, and as there was no room available to practice at home, he had decided to "escape" to school to practice. Finally, I had to know why Boris had chosen to play the piece so slowly when it would take forever to finish it at that tempo. He explained to me that his father had told him to practice the piece like that. I was very surprised.[2]

Boris would begin practicing the piece by using an entire bow length for each note, playing at a very slow, unchanging tempo (I had caught him at this initial stage of practicing). Once he'd finished the piece in this manner (which took about two hours), he would begin again using half a bow length, doubling the speed. After this he would move to quarter bow lengths, and so on and so forth until he reached the final tempo.

"How long does it take you to practice the piece?" I asked. "Approximately four to five hours," he responded. I was speechless. Boris explained to me that practicing this way helped him to develop a very good bow technique, as well as to memorize the piece. He turned back to his music and resumed his practicing.

His musical career would show that Boris did indeed develop very solid technique. He would go on to win the prestigious

---

2 *Perpetual Motion* was written to be performed with a very fast bouncing bow stroke called 'spiccato,' played in the middle of the bow and at the required tempo, so that it would take no longer than three minutes to play from start to finish.

Paganini competition and later served as concertmaster with several European orchestras.

Some Sundays I went to visit my relatives. My father had two brothers. The oldest, Jacob, lived in Frunze with his family. The youngest, David, was injured in the war, and while recovering in the hospital, had met a nurse named Elena who became his wife. She lived in Moscow, and David found his new home in the big city.

To get to my uncle David's place I had to take a subway, change trains three times, and then walk for fifteen minutes. Usually I would visit him on Sunday, when the trains were less full and I could manage to find a seat.

They lived in a one-bedroom apartment with their grown son and two small dogs. Whenever I visited they always served dinner, and it felt a bit like being at home. The worst part for me was after dinner when Elena started playing with the dogs, who loved to lick her lips. I could not imagine why humans would do that, and shuddered at the thought of them licking my lips. It was awkward and painful to watch, but she had fun, God bless her.

People who live in Moscow are really proud of their city. To be more precise, they are proud of themselves for living in the biggest Russian city, once the capital of the Soviet Union. It is a privilege to be called *Moscvitch* (so much so that even a Russian automobile was named "Moscvitch"). People who live in Moscow feel like they are an elite class. There is only one other city in Russia that has the guts to compare itself with Moscow in terms of that elite feeling, and that is St. Petersburg. The people of St. Petersburg look down at *Moscvitchi* as nonintellectuals, and *Moscvitchi* in turn consider St. Petersburg, which was once the capital of Russia, a cultural suburb.

Moscow has its own architecture. Its style was shaped by Stalin when he ordered a set of seven tall buildings, sometimes referred to as The Seven Sisters, to be erected around the city. There is nothing like it in any other Russian city. Stalin's skyscrapers became another manifestation of his power and of Russian force. Moscow also has a number of beautiful parks, but I never really felt safe in them, even in the daytime.

In front of the Bolshoi Theatre there was a large square with a charming park. Trees, lilac bushes, and plenty of flowers created a wonderful atmosphere that became more intimate after sunset. There was a lot of activity in the square during the day, and one could see people laughing and talking, always in a good mood. It was also the place where gay people went to meet one another. Gay people were always persecuted in Russia; first by the church, then by the communists who believed that they came from the devil. Homosexuality was considered a perversion that could not and should not survive in a progressive socialist society.

In college we knew that some of our friends had a different sexual orientation, but nobody would speak aloud about it. And none of us felt comfortable walking across that park, especially when it was getting dark, as that was the time when the *militzia* would make raids and arrest people. These "cleansings" happened on a regular basis, but gay people did not want to give up. The next day they would come back again in a silent protest against communist oppression. And everything would start again.

My violin teacher, Julia Breitburg, had a lot of passion for teaching. We had our regular lessons at school and additional lessons at her apartment. She was a good teacher, but after two years I felt stuck. I tried hard, but could not really understand her style and demands. A new rule which limited hours of teaching for part-time teachers (she was one of them) went into effect, and I was moved to a different teacher. It was a good transition for me.

Sergei Madatov was a very talented violinist. He had served as concertmaster in major Moscow orchestras, but he had a rebellious character. One time during a lesson he suggested an exceptionally good bowing at the opening of Lalo's *Symphony Espagnole*, emphatically waving the cigarette that never left his fingers. At the time I was preparing that same piece for a final exam. I tried his suggestions and the passage instantly grew vibrant and energetic. I loved it, but his response was, "Playing these bowings for the jury would be like throwing pearls in front of swine." With such a sharp tongue, it was no wonder he could not hold jobs for long. He was the teacher who fanned my flame of curiosity about music, style, bowings, and good fingerings. He built in me a foundation for the lifelong courage to experiment, keep an open mind, and discover new things. In the one year that I studied with him, I learned not only how to be a better violinist and musician, but a better human being. In my college years I would often visit him at home, and when he became sick, I helped him with chores.

Our Russian literature teacher was an old woman, very kind and charming. She radiated serenity and love. When I was in her class I started reading significantly more, and ever since those days I hear her voice whenever I pick up a book. At the time, my favorite was Dostoevsky's *Crime and Punishment*, which I read in two days. Though I enjoyed Leo Tolstoy's short stories, I was glad that his epic four-volume *War and Peace* was not mandatory reading. I would never have been able to complete such an assignment. I really feel sorry for Tolstoy's wife who had to rewrite this gigantic novel three times by hand!

My math teacher, a middle-aged man, wore glasses with very thick lenses. His eyesight was so bad that he had to bring the textbook right under his nose to read it. But we had a feeling that he could see all of us, especially during exams, when some of us shamelessly tried to cheat. He would stare at us hypnotically, and it was impossible to figure out who was in his angle of observation. He appreciated out-of-the-box thinking, and when he gave us a problem to solve, he would become very excited if a student found a way to answer it in an unusual way. He would jump to grab the class grade book and give an automatic "A" to that lucky pupil. A couple of times I happened to be that student. One time he even disregarded some of my earlier poorer grades, and gave me an "A" as a semester grade, far before the semester's end. Even though I liked my math teacher a lot, I cannot say that I was in love with mathematics. However, I've always been adept at mental math. I still impress my kids when it comes to doing calculations in my mind, and often can do them in less time than it takes for them to reach for their fancy calculators.

We had many music classes, and in addition, a full spectrum of other disciplines: history, geography, physics, and chemistry – in other words, everything that "normal" kids study at "normal" schools. How did we manage to do all that homework and find the time to practice hours and hours on our instruments? Youthful energy was probably the key.

Our class was the smallest in the school. Only twelve kids

remained in my class after the "pruning" at the end of the eighth grade. When I joined the class, I became the youngest, a tough situation to be in. It was a time of hormonal upheaval, but I was too young to be of any interest to the girls in my class. Some girls, like the very attractive Irina, had no problem procuring admirers. She was skinny and elegant with a special green fog in her eyes. One look at those eyes made me tremble like a leaf on a tree in a storm. She was nice to me, but that did not promise anything. I was cute (as I was told) but unpopular, and did not have anything to offer at that time. I had no idea how to talk to girls, and did not know what they wanted. One day a girl with the beautiful name of Nadezhda (which means hope) who was one class above me brought me a portrait she'd drawn of me. It was drawn in pencil, and she was obviously talented. Looking back, I now understand that she must have liked me, but I totally missed her cues. I still have the portrait.

My portrait by Nadezhda

I did not have any real friends at school, but became close with a double bass player named Sergei Gorbunov. He was in love with his large instrument, and there was quite a contrast in mentality between the violinist and the double bass player. We often argued, trying to resolve all of the world's problems and find the meaning of life. Sergei practiced all day long, and his hands became very strong. They looked like they were made out of rubber and metal, and I would not ever think of getting in a fight with him, even as a joke. He became an outstanding player and later joined a major symphony orchestra in Moscow.

There was one girl I liked a lot. Regina was a year younger than me, and actually paid attention to me. She was lovely; her dark eyes drilled into me, hypnotizing me. She played harp, and since her harp did not fit in the elevator, I often got to play the role of the strong man when it came to moving her harp from the classroom where she practiced to the recital hall on the upper level. The stairs had big steps, and my muscles were getting stronger by the day with each trip. Our relationship remained strictly platonic, but I concluded that in the future it would be better to date violinists because their instruments weren't as heavy.

The famous Russian Museum of Fine Arts was named after neither painter nor sculptor, but oddly after the great Russian poet Alexander Pushkin. The museum was just a few blocks away from the place where I lived, and I often stood in long lines of people to get to the entry doors. The line looked like a snake curling around the block and stretching into the neighboring street. Two to three hours in line was normal if you wanted to see a rare exhibition. I started to attend the concerts, but my funds were limited, and despite the low entrance fee for students, I could not afford it on a regular basis. Moscow was blooming with wonderful performances, and I would enjoy them more after joining the college. Meanwhile I was lucky enough to attend a few operas and ballets at the Bolshoi Theatre, and witnessed the amazingly flexible hands of Maya Plisetskaya, one of the most famous Russian ballerinas of the second half of the 20th century, dancing her immortal *Swan* by Saint-Saëns.

In the spring of 1970 I attended for the first time as an audience member the fourth Tchaikovsky International Competition and started collecting autographs of all the distinguished musical judges. The prestigious violin jury included David Oistrakh, Arthur Grumiaux, Leonid Kogan, Joseph Szigeti, and Efrem Zimbalist, among others. I still have a brochure from one competition with photographs and the list of pieces every violinist performed during the three rounds, along with my comments. One of the basic rules of the competition was that all music had to be memorized. But in the first round, one of the contestants came on stage with a music stand, put his music on it, and started to play Bach's *Adagio* for solo violin. We could not believe our eyes. The jury let him finish the piece and then David Oistrakh, through the interpreter (the player was a foreigner), asked the violinist why he was performing with music. Without a shadow of embarrassment, the violinist responded that he did not have enough time to memorize it. It sounded like a joke, since practically every violinist learns that

Adagio at school and memorizes it. By the way, that violinist played it badly. He obviously did not have enough time to memorize nor learn the piece well. The intonation was not clean, a lot of rhythms were performed incorrectly, and to me he appeared to have been sight-reading. Of course, the musician was disqualified from further participation.

But there were many good violinists. Twenty-two year-old Glenn Dicterow represented the United States of America. He played well and the comment I wrote in my program read, "Gifted violinist." At the age of 31, he became the concertmaster of the New York Philharmonic, the youngest violinist ever appointed to that position. He held the post for 34 years, becoming the longest-serving concertmaster of that prestigious orchestra. Elmar Oliveira impressed me with super precise octaves in the Paganini *Capriccios*. After the competition, he made a good career as a soloist, and I would both hear and play with him a few times in the 1990s when he came to Seattle. There was a young violinist from Finland, Ilkka Talvi, who would become the concertmas-

4th Tchaikovsky International Competition Pamphlet Cover

ter of the Seattle Symphony 20 some years later, and with whom I would share the stage for quite a few years. I liked the Japanese violinist Mayumi Fujikawa for the quality of her performance and for her absolute control, especially in super challenging virtuoso pieces. A very strong team of Soviet violinists consistently led the competition: Nana Jashvili, Liana Isakadze, Andrei Korsakov, and Tatyana Grindenko. The audience fell in love with the sweet and charming sounds of Vladimir Spivakov. His bright presentation of Rodion Shchedrin's *Humoresque* and *In the Style of Albeniz* created thunderous applause and brought Spivakov the second prize, which he shared with Fujikawa. The first prize unanimously went to 23-year-old Gidon Kremer. Along with other pieces he performed, I remember his brilliant and haunting rendition of the extremely virtuosic *Last Rose of Summer* by Heinrich Ernst. All of these incredibly talented players would go on to have prominent solo careers. Thirty some years later I would hear Gidon Kremer with his ensemble Kremerata Baltica in concert in Seattle. All the musicians played standing and gave a memorable performance of Piazzolla's *Seasons* with Kremer as soloist.

The Tchaikovsky Competition was and remains the major musical event in Russia. Founded in 1958, it is held in Moscow every four years. It attracts the best young musicians from all over the world. Victory at this competition means receiving a substantial monetary prize, but more importantly, it means a lucky ticket that opens doors to the concert stage for solo performances with orchestras as well as recordings. In 1982 and 1986 as part of the Moscow State Symphony I accompanied the pianists, violinists, and cellists in the final rounds of the competition. In each of three rounds there was a different mandatory piece for the players. In the final round it was always Tchaikovsky's First Piano Concerto, his Violin Concerto, and *Variations on a Rococo Theme* for the cello. We would play those pieces a dozen times at the rehearsals and a dozen times at the actual competition. One can imagine that after so many repetitions we had our orchestra parts memorized!

The Grand Hall of the Moscow Conservatory and Tchaikovsky Concert Hall were the places where most of the competitions took place, and in those days one could find all the classical music lovers of the city eager to hear the new rising stars. The streets around the halls looked like a beehive on those days. During the competition it was practically impossible to get tickets; everything was sold out far in advance, and there was always a big crowd in front of the entrance asking for any available ticket.

The Tchaikovsky Concert Hall could brag about neither its acoustics nor its architecture, but the Grand Hall of the Conservatory was the perfect venue. It was inaugurated in 1901 and has only recently had its first major renovation, almost 110 years later. The hall was sometimes called "an enormous Stradivarius violin" for its remarkable acoustics. Framed oval portraits of the great composers with serious and gloomy faces (Beethoven looked the angriest) looked down at people from the walls as if they were saying, "We are the real judges!" The level of competition was so high that many times no one was awarded first place. After each round I rushed back home to practice, inspired by the wonderful players I had heard. Many of them I would hear two decades later in the United States; some would become real stars and be propelled to the top of the artistic world. Some never grew up, and simply played the same few pieces they had learned at the conservatory over and over again, sounding less and less exciting with each repetition. Attending that memorable fourth Tchaikovsky Competition was a great educational experience for my 15-year-old self. I also attended a few of the subsequent Tchaikovsky Competitions, but there was an obvious decline in the quality of violinists coming to this major music festival. I could see that the reason for this was the general decline of Russian instrumental performance, a trend that I will discuss later.

Three years at school passed quickly, and soon it was time to spread my wings and fly on to the next level. I started to prepare for a new phase in my life – musical college – but first, I had a whole lot of practicing to do.

10 · Gnessin State Musical College

It was one of the hottest summers Moscow had ever had. The city was surrounded by turf swamps, and when the temperature reached a critical point, the turf would start to burn under the surface. Since the fire started underground, it was basically impossible to stop it from happening. Clouds of dark smelly smoke surrounded Moscow all summer long. When the wind started blowing toward the city, the air pollution became unbearable. Masks would not have helped, not that people had any. There was no choice but to leave the city. The smoke would diminish after the temperature went down.

That summer I was preparing to take an entrance exam for the prestigious Gnessin Musical College. My family decided that they would provide support for me during that stressful time, so my father flew to Moscow to stay with me during exams. Unfortunately, it ended up being the other way around. Upon his arrival in Moscow he got sick, so sick that he had to be admitted to the hospital. He had terrible headaches, dizziness, and was afraid he was dying. The doctors diagnosed him with a minor stroke. After each exam, I would rush to the hospital and deliver the good news: another "A"! That would make him feel a little better for a moment, but I couldn't calm his fear of dying while so far away from home. After my final exam (I aced all of them), he slowly started feeling better, got more stable, and soon was able to walk. We flew back home. The remaining days of summer passed quickly, and suddenly I was back again on the plane, this time as a college student.

For the first time in my life I was to live in a dormitory. I was excited but a bit scared. I shared a room with three other fellows: a choral conductor, a bayanist (bayan is the Russian version of accordion), and another violinist. The bayanist was a virtuoso and practiced many hours each day in our room. Though he played brilliantly, the sound of the bayan soon became very annoying when I heard it all the time from a couple of feet away. The violinist was a nice guy and a very talented musician. At the age of 19 he was already married and had a baby. We were both assigned to the same classes and got along just fine.

The choral conductor was an alcoholic. Sometimes we had to take care of him, since he drank to an absolutely senseless condition. Once, upon my return to the dormitory after class, I tried to open the door to our room, helplessly turning the key and knob. The door would not open. Then I realized that the door was actually unlocked. I pushed it as hard as I could. My roommate's body was blocking it from the other side, and it took me a while to enter the room. He looked like he was dead, but I was already accustomed to his "tricks." His body was so heavy that I could only drag him by his feet, finally depositing him on his bed. I was exhausted and covered in sweat. The moment I turned to close the door, I heard a thud. He had turned over without waking up and landed on the floor. I gave up.

As I understand it now, our dormitory was no different from any other (I learned this after both of my kids told me stories about the dormitories they lived in during their college years). There were some differences, however. From the outside people could hear that the building was filled with noise machines, blending in a horrible cacophony. We practiced literally all day long. One might compare this noise with that of a symphony orchestra warming up before a concert. Except in this case, all of us were trying to prove the exceptional qualities we possessed multiplied by the power of our giant college-aged egos. Mastering passages required tons of energy and strong fingers. We all had them, and we were all very aware of the theory of the survival of the fittest.

This does not mean that we didn't have fun. One can imagine what kind of fun we could have, just having come through our final years of puberty. Almost everybody drank quite heavily, but if there was drug use, I remained unaware of it. Our dinners consisted of a bottle of vodka and a couple of beers as a starter. The main dish was heavily buttered noodles served in a big pot, steaming and spreading an incredible aroma that only warm bread and warm noodles can. We slept well after such dinners, so well that one day when I came to my violin lesson and opened my case, I discovered it was empty. I had left my violin back home on the piano where I had put it after finishing my practicing the day before.

In those days, violence on the streets of Moscow was a fact of life. It wasn't unusual to see people fighting each other on the street, and nobody ever reported them. Fights and robberies were so routine that a group of students including myself started a martial arts club in the dormitory basement. Though I never had the chance to use my minor skills on the street, lifting weights and general fitness helped me to build up my body. It became a lifelong habit, and there is not a single day that I forego my exercise. The guy who was the instructor for our club was a singer with a super strong body, a modest version of Arnold Schwarzenegger.

One day when I entered the building, I knew something was wrong. The entrance lobby looked quite different. There was blood on the floor and the walls, and people were screaming. I saw a guy holding a knife running around, bleeding like a fountain. Our martial arts teacher grabbed and disarmed him. He put his fingers on the guy's carotid artery and pressed hard. The bleeding stopped, and soon an ambulance arrived. He survived despite losing a lot of blood. Nobody knew what had happened. Maybe he just went nuts and accidentally hurt himself. This was not uncommon in our high-pressure environment. Another time a girl jumped out of a window, and yet another day we could not enter the dormitory because the police (in those days, the *militzia*) had blocked the entrance to our building. The news leaked out that there was a case of syphilis at the college. The militzia were trying to catch the girl who was suspected of having syphilis and isolate her. They succeeded, and when they left the building, I recognized the girl. I don't recall if she ever came back.

Bed bugs were a big problem, and it was almost impossible to get rid of them. The most reliable way to resolve the problem was to burn the mattress filled with bugs which only created a new problem: how to get a new mattress. The dormitory had no extras.

On New Year's Eve we celebrated in our own way. At midnight exactly, timed with the last beat of the Kremlin Tower clock, we drunkenly opened our doors and smashed our empty liquor bottles against the walls of the hallway. It would be a great test for a distinguished yogi to walk barefoot in the corridor after such a memorable night. I don't remember who cleaned up the mess afterwards.

It took me an average of fifty minutes to an hour to get from my dormitory to the college. The nearest subway station was a

ten-minute walk. Once on the subway, I would change trains twice
before the brisk fifteen-minute walk to the college. I could forego
the walk and take a bus instead, but waiting for it could take more
than fifteen minutes, and one could never rely on its capricious
schedule. I went to college every day, and travelling by subway on
weekdays was often a nightmare. Of course at the time, I accepted
it as an ordinary part of my days; only looking back do I realize
how insane it was!

The Moscow subway opened in 1935 and was one of the most
unique and ambitious Soviet architectural projects in the history
of the USSR. No two stations look alike, and many of them are
truly beautiful. Despite the city's strict passport control, Moscow's
population grew rapidly, and the subway became the city's most
popular and reliable mode of public transportation and remains as
such, carrying millions of people every day.

During peak travel times simply entering the station proved to
be a feat of endurance. Nestled in a sea of commuters like sardines
in a tin, one moved at the speed of a tortoise down the stairway
to the trains. The trickiest part involved actually getting onto the
train. The crowd, a powerful human wave, moved independently
with a life of its own, and if you were lucky, its movement would
literally push you through the train's open doors.

Once aboard, I always feared for the safety of my violin. The
case was not strong enough to withstand the pressure from people's
bodies and could easily be crushed, damaging my precious (but in-
expensive) instrument. To prevent this from happening, I would
hold the violin upright and in front of me and jut my elbows out a
bit, creating a protective shield. My top priority at the time was to
find a more durable case to avoid this continued stress.

Someone once told me that in Tokyo there are people hired
specifically to push passengers through the doors of the trains during rush hour so that the doors can close properly. In Moscow there
was no need to hire anybody for this job. There were always volunteers behind you who would gladly shove you into the cars with all
their might! This created an entirely new challenge: getting off at
your stop. It wasn't always possible, especially if you didn't already
happen to be near the doors. If you missed your stop, you would
simply have to try your luck at the next one. If you were fortunate

enough to get shoved into the right train, you would ride it back to your stop and continue on your merry way.

I was fortunate and honored to be accepted into the class of the most famous teacher in the college, Professor Piotr Bondarenko. He was already an old man, probably in his late 70's, and had a sweet smile. He called all of his students *detochka*, a nickname which means "child." Despite his age, he worked a lot. For many years he was the only assistant to the Russian violin superstar David Oistrakh, and when he traveled around the world on tour, Bondarenko taught not only his own student class at the Gnessin College, but also all of Oistrakh's students at the conservatory. This worked out to more than 30 students twice a week, plus unlimited lessons at his home.

The doors of the professor's apartment were never closed. Students came in and out all day long. One time I came to take an additional lesson in his apartment. Since the doors were not locked, I entered without knocking. There were a few rooms in the apartment, and I tried to locate the professor. Violin sounds were coming from all of the rooms. I opened the first door but he was not there. I opened the second door and was shocked to see Gidon Kremer practicing there with his wife, Tatyana Grindenko, a gorgeous woman and a wonderful violinist. At that time, they were both already winners of international competitions, and yet here they were, still coming for a lesson with the professor.

But the lessons, to be honest, were not that exciting. Most of the time the professor would tap the rhythm on a table with a big piece of wood attached to a classroom key. This is what was happening behind the doors to famous room No. 89! From time to time the professor would fall asleep and the rhythm of the key would slow down. At the moment it stopped, the professor would lift his head and resume the beat, sometimes out of sync with our rhythm. We had to adjust. He did not speak much. The lesson usually started with his greeting, *"Zdravstvuy, detochka.* What are you going to play today?" and often ended up with, "You know what to do at home?" (I nodded my head.) "So go home and practice." My curious mind wanted more of a challenge. I wanted to experiment and try things that might cause me trouble. I would ask, "Professor, can we try some different bowings or fingerings?" The answer was always the same: "*Detochka*, if something will not be right, I will tell you."

The professor's specialty was his low "C". No, am not talking about the grade, but about the note "C-natural". Let me explain myself. Let's assume that you are playing the violin. If you press your left hand's second finger on the A string, you will get the note "C". This is not a difficult note to find on the fingerboard, especially after playing the violin for 12 years. The problem was that the professor heard this note lower than any of his students. How many times did I hear, "Note 'C' is too high, *detochka*." Of course all of his students had to lower that damn note to satisfy him. Since most of us had perfect pitch, it was quite painful to play what sounded wrong to us. It was almost like playing out of tune on purpose. I spent four years in his class, and I think that the professor's greatest merit was that he did not allow us to go in the wrong direction (except for that low "C"). In music, this might be crucial for young players, and I have seen a few violinists whose artistic development rapidly declined once they lost the right guidance.

A pianist was always present in the class, waiting patiently to accompany us while we executed scales and etudes. The lesson would run for 45 minutes, and often we were advised to audit other students' lessons. It was a good way to learn in advance what pieces we might play next. That's where I first saw and heard the beautiful brunette, Alla. She would become my wife a few years later.

As a straight-A student, I received a stipend of 40 rubles per month (the stipend I would lose after an unfortunate political economy exam). Obviously my appetites often went far beyond this modest student salary. I found a wonderful job that made me feel like a rich man. Moscow had and still has an excellent Operetta Theater. People always filled the house. Only the best operettas were performed: Strauss' *Die Fledermaus*, *The Merry Widow* by Lehar, Kalman's *Countess Maritza*, and others of the same caliber. This great music had one important quality: it made people happy. It made me happy too when I joined the orchestra for five rubles a show. A violinist was needed and I was hired to play every night. By the end of the first month of my employment, I was promoted to the concertmaster position and made 150 rubles in my first month. Now I could afford to take a taxi and to have more sophisticated dinners than those I described earlier. My life got brighter, but I started to neglect my practicing, which did not go unnoticed. Professor Bondarenko had many years of experience dealing with students, and one time after I played my scales he asked me directly if I had started working. I had to admit that he had guessed right. He explained tersely that I had two choices: to study with him and quit working, or continue working and be expelled from his class. My choice was obvious.

At the end of the 1970s, thousands and thousands of Russian Jews were leaving the country to seek a better life in the free world. Just before my last year at college our professor told us that he was going to immigrate to Israel. That's how I found myself in the class of Nelli Shkolnikova. I knew her as a brilliant violinist, one of the

Gnessin Musical College, Class of Professor Bondarenko

first and best of her generation along with Albert Markov, who also taught at Gnessin College. They both were former students of Yuri Yankelevich, a legendary violin teacher at the Moscow Conservatory. Later on more wonderful violinists graduated from his class: Tretyakov, Spivakov, and others.

Nelli Efimovna (that is what we called her) was a superb teacher. During the lesson she would often ask, "Misha, do you understand how to play this passage?" Sometimes I was embarrassed to admit that I was not quick enough to grasp the ideas she shared with me. She would see that I did not understand, and we would start over. Feeling even more embarrassed when the task was too difficult, I would say, "Nelli Efimovna, I will practice this more at home and I will understand it." Her response was, "Misha, if you don't understand what I am trying to explain to you, that means that I am not a good teacher," and she would start all over again until I really understood what needed to be done.

At our first lesson she asked me, "What are you going to play?" Before leaving for summer vacation, all students were assigned many etudes and other pieces to practice during the three month break. (At that time I *did* practice during the summer.) I had a big list from Professor Bondarenko. My favorite was the Beethoven Violin Concerto, and I practiced that marvelous music a lot. I replied, "The Beethoven Violin Concerto." How could I have known that this was the same concerto Shkolnikova first performed when she was forty? She felt that she was not musically mature enough to play this simple but very difficult music any earlier. "Please start," she said, and I dived into those elegant octaves. I hadn't yet finished the second bar when she stopped me and said, "Misha, would you play a scale, please?" And at that moment I started to learn to play the violin from scratch, like I had never played it before. An interesting thing happened right away – I found that "C" note which I mentioned earlier. Miraculously, it was exactly in the place I expected it to be. Not lower, but precisely right there. Many more discoveries followed. Shkolnikova opened a whole new world to me and in one year with her I learned more than in all previous years at the college. She was an outstanding teacher and, as Russians say, she could teach a rabbit to play the violin.

I was lucky to have some really great teachers at the college. One of them, Jaroslav Aleksandrov, was my string quartet teacher. At the time he played with the world-famous Borodin String Quartet. He was a man from a different planet. He played on a unique and gorgeous violin made some 300 years ago by Nicolo Amati, the teacher of Antonio Stradivari and Giuseppe Guarneri. These names are iconic in the musical world, and it is the dream of any instrumentalist if not to own such an instrument (they are extremely expensive), then at least to play one once in their lifetime. At the time I did not dare ask to even touch such a treasure. If somebody had told me that 30 years later I would be allowed to play on such superb violins, I would have thought it was a bad joke.

I fell in love with the string quartet as a unique experience where one could showcase his musical and technical abilities while at the same time having an intelligent, musically philosophical conversation with his colleagues. We studied quartets by Haydn, Mozart, Beethoven, Brahms, and of course, Shostakovich. His quartet No. 8 was our favorite. Its official dedication is "to the victims of fascism," but in reality, everybody knew his quartet was dedicated to the six million Russian Jews murdered by fascists. This was manifested in the screaming klezmer theme at the climax of the quartet. The Russian government would never allow this piece to be performed with such a dedication to the memory of Holocaust victims. We were so obsessed with that deeply tragic music that we literally could not stop practicing. Often we had our rehearsals at our cellist's apartment. Igor was older than the rest of us and was married. His wife was so nice that at each break (and we practiced for hours!), she would offer us food and tea, so we could refill our energy and continue on our quartet voyage.

Each lesson with Aleksandrov was like a holiday for me and my colleagues. I played first violin, and loved to do the bowings for the whole quartet. It became so much fun for me that later I would volunteer to do the bowings for all of the strings in the orchestras I conducted. Reading a musical score became like reading a book for me, except much more thrilling. I liked to see the relationships between the notes, lines, and instruments, and to see how the composer used them to create magnificent sounds. It was at that time I realized that I wanted to stretch my skills as a musician and play the "biggest instrument," the orchestra itself.

Meanwhile, our quartet made such progress that at some point our teacher suggested that we form our own group, and build our careers with our string quartet. This was a serious suggestion coming from a world-renowned musician. We were flattered, and debates followed. We knew how the Borodin Quartet practiced. Every day they met at the studio and spent five hours of intense practicing with a couple of ten minutes breaks in between. We knew how difficult it was to maintain good relationships within the quartet and how easily quarrels could break it apart. We also realized that competing with similar groups might not be realistic for us for many reasons, and how difficult it might be to make a living as a string quartet player. We decided to remain good friends.

On many occasions I had the opportunity to observe the classes of the legendary cellist Valentin Berlinsky, who was also a member of the Borodin Quartet. (Students were not allowed to take lessons from other teachers except the ones we were assigned to, so I could only observe.) Berlinsky demonstrated exciting techniques on his amazing cello. Our favorite was when he played countless different types of pizzicato (plucking of the string). Every pizzicato was different and reflected the character of the music. It was like drawing a picture with many colors, and he did not even use his bow. His bow could make the cello sing and cry and roar. Hundreds of characters came alive, rising before us when he played. After Berlinsky I never heard anyone who could make the cello sound like a whole new world. We were in the presence of a Great Master. I came to the conclusion that still remains unchanged that the cello is the most natural among all instruments and comes closest to the human voice. However, I loved my violin and would not exchange it for any other instrument, even the cello.

In addition to the musical disciplines we had a few classes that everybody understood were absolutely unnecessary for our future, but there was no getting around taking them. They included the History of the Communist Party of the USSR, Russian Folk Art, Civil Defense, and the Political Economy of Socialism and Capitalism. The teacher for the History of the Party liked me and always gave me an "A". The Political Economy class turned out to be a difficult one. That teacher was not my favorite. I aced the capitalism part (for some reason it was easy for me to understand how the capitalist economy worked), but got stuck on the socialist part of the course. I could not see the logic in the system. I got a "C" on the exam, and lost my stipend. I had been a straight-A student up to that point.

The funniest class was probably the Civil Defense class, but not because of the subject. The subject was not a joke at all. This was a time of very tense relations between the USSR and the US, and both countries were preparing their citizens for possible nuclear war. The fun part was the teacher, but not in the way you might suspect. He was a former military officer, and had zero knowledge about music. During his (very boring) class, the door of the classroom would sometimes swing open and a student would stick his head in and announce, "Kirill Ivanovich, we need a string quartet for the rehearsal now." The teacher understood the importance of the request, and in military tone ordered, "String quartet, to the rehearsal!" Five or six people would get up and leave. Another time it was even more hilarious. The door opened and the student said, "Kirill Ivanovich, the truck with flats and sharps just arrived. Volunteers are needed to unload the truck." "Who will volunteer?" the professor asked. A few people raised their hands and left the room.

On my final violin exam, I performed a program of Paganini, Szymanowski and my favorite Shostakovich First Violin Concerto. I graduated with all four top degrees: teacher, orchestra player, chamber musician, and soloist.

My hunger for music was growing and needed to be satisfied. I started to collect sheet music, scores, and records. All of the money left after food expenses went to the music store. I still have a wonderful collection of first-rate sheet music, which was quite easy for me to buy at that time.

Melodiya was the only record label in the Soviet Union at that time. They produced a wide variety of recordings from Soviet artists, and was obviously OK'd by the Ministry of Culture. *Melodiya* became far busier when some Russian artists "forgot" about their loyalty to the system and began to emigrate to the West. Because of their "betrayal," their recordings were pulled from the shelves and destroyed. In some cases, in an attempt to not waste money, their names would simply be erased from the labels on the vinyl, after which they would continue to be sold. For example, one could buy a recording of viola music played by Rudolf Barshai but his name would be nowhere on the record. Likewise, a record of the Moscow Philharmonic Orchestra performing under the conductor Kirill Kondrashin would have appeared to have no conductor at all. Of course none of these musicians ever received any royalties since Russian musicians were paid for recordings only by the minute. This lump sum was all the payment they would ever receive.

All profits from later copies of the recordings went directly into the hands of the government.

I didn't know that for all those years, *Melodiya* had shamelessly been reprinting recordings from multiple foreign studios (mostly American), infringing on international copyright laws. Similar fraudulent activity was happening with literature as well as visual art. None of the foreign artists ever saw any of their royalties from the Russian government. One upside to this was that Russian music lovers were able to have access to the best of classical and jazz from all over the world.

All the while my record collection continued to grow and now included a lot of instrumentalists and singers, symphonic and choral groups. In the excitement of my youth, I continued to discover an amazing world of classical music, devouring practically everything that arrived in the store.

There was only one record store in Moscow, perfectly situated near the Moscow Conservatory. In a small dusty room filled with hundreds of records, one could find music fanatics browsing with deep concentration. These people owned all the possible records and knew everything there was to know about every musician in the world. They were always in front of the store long before the doors opened at 10:00 in the morning, eager to get their hands on a new limited edition of an album from labels of other socialist countries, most frequently Poland, Hungary, or the German Democratic Republic.[3]

A few recordings in particular got my attention. One was Leonard Bernstein with Shostakovich's Fifth Symphony. I found what Bernstein did with the classical Russian symphony to be refreshingly unusual. We knew this symphony very well from the fine

---

3 At that time, the Soviet Union did not have any sort of musical trade with capitalist countries because the Russian ruble could not buy anything from the capitalist market. It was not recognized by the world market as equal currency to so-called "firm" currencies such as the US dollar, French franc, or English pound. In fact, we used to jokingly refer to the Russian ruble as "soft" currency. The Soviet newspaper *Izvestiya* (translation: *News*) published a weekly table comparing the ruble to other currencies of the world. Soviet people would look at the table and, with great satisfaction, see that the US dollar, reported to be worth only 90 kopeks, was always weaker than the ruble. At some point when America's volatile economy experienced a normal downturn, the dollar fell to just 70 kopeks. This was cause for celebration among the Russian people. Long live the Russian economy, the most stable economy in the world!

renditions by the major Russian conductors, the epitome of which was Mravinsky with his Leningrad Philharmonic. Mravinsky knew Shostakovich personally and prepared his music following the composer's every detailed wish to a T. On the contrary, Bernstein took quite a few liberties with tempo and pacing and this proved shocking to the Russian ear. No one had dared to play Shostakovich in Russia like this. It took me quite a while to realize it but I came to the conclusion that Bernstein's perceived "freshness" was in fact no more than a desire for originality and had no artistic ground. I haven't liked that recording since. This also brought the following question to mind: how much freedom should one be allowed when interpreting classical music? And how successful do such experiments tend to be?

Contrary to Bernstein's questionable treatment of Shostakovich's masterpiece, the following musicians were able to retain the integrity of the original music while infusing it with their own magic. Wilhelm Furtwangler's special talent was the ability to craft remarkably long phrases in Wagner's music. This consisted of following the flow of the melody, sculpting it along the way into a honeyed, sustained phrase. No one could compare to this extraordinary German conductor who, despite having somewhat lousy technique and remarkably slow tempos, was able to create an absolutely hypnotizing effect on his audience. Pablo Casals considered Bach's Cello Suites to be the bible of music. There is so much depth and wisdom to the music and especially to his interpretation. Casals believed that this music had a purifying effect on the soul, and because of this he played one or two movements from the suites every single day of his life up to the age of ninety-six when he could no longer hold his bow. Another phenomenal cellist, Emanuel Feuermann, struck me with the most incredible singing quality of his instrument. I had never heard another cellist (or any instrumentalist) who could make their instrument sing more beautifully than Feuermann. However, the interpretation that has had the most impact on me by far has been Yehudi Menuhin's out of this world rendition of Beethoven's Violin Concerto (the second movement in particular). When I listen to this recording I feel that it's not a violin being played, but the voice of God communicating to us mortals about the enormous beauty of the world in which we live.

Moscow was and still is the center of cultural life in the country. Like a magnet, it sucked in all the best brains and talent from the farthest parts of the Russian empire. People wanted to hear and see the best cultural achievements, and in Moscow they could have them every day. I attended numerous concerts at the conservatory, both in the Grand Hall and at the smaller Recital Hall. The entrance fee for students was 50 kopeks (about 50 cents) to stand for the whole concert on the very top of the second amphitheater. There was no air-conditioning, and in the summertime you would not want to stand so close to the ceiling. I could not care less. I was on top of the world. I was so lucky to hear the best musicians of that time, Russian as well as guest artists from all over the world. David Oistrakh, Yehudi Menuhin, Vladimir Horowitz, Leonid Kogan, Sviatoslav Richter, Mstislav Rostropovich, and many others played for us.

Foreign artists came to Moscow for different reasons. Some of them were curious about Russian culture; some may have been sympathetic to the ideas of our society, who knows? But Russian audiences, as many of these musicians stated, were the most excited and grateful audiences they ever had.

I will forever remember the concert of Yehudi Menuhin, whom we knew only by a few records that had reached Moscow music stores. One day a rumor spread among college students that the next morning the conservatory's box office would open at 10 a.m. to sell tickets for Menuhin's concert. For such unique concerts people would stand in line all night to make sure they could buy a ticket. It was winter time, and around 10 p.m. I went to the conservatory with a plan to spend the night waiting for the box office to open. I put on all my warmest clothes, got a heavy stick in case I had to fight off hooligans, and began to wait. Somewhere around midnight the *militzioner* went by and noticed me warming up at the telephone booth. "What are you doing here at night?" he asked in a threatening voice. I explained, and he let me be. He knew what I was talking about. The cold was unbearable. I tried to jump and jog, but stayed close to the booth because if I got too far away someone else might take it. Around 2 a.m., I noticed that I was still the only one "in line." That made me suspicious, but I reassured myself that the lazier, less committed people would come around 5-6 a.m. That was a long and cold night. To keep warm I paced in circles around the Tchaikovsky monument that was situated in the small park in front of the Moscow conservatory. The Russian composer sat comfortably in a big chair that seemed more like a throne. A pile of snow atop his head served as a crown and his expression made him appear lost in thought. As I jogged to and fro in front of his namesake conservatory, I couldn't help but feel his suspicious gaze on me. By morning, we were both tired but he never did take his eyes off of me. The sun rose, and I did not see any people coming. I continued to wait. People went by, the first bus came, but nobody wanted to form a line with me. At 10 a.m. the box office opened, and I felt very happy to be the first one, only to learn that the tickets would be going on sale the following day.

I made it to the concert and it was remarkable. To us, Menuhin was an enigma. He practiced yoga, and could play the violin in the lotus position. He was a legend, especially because of the mysterious disease that affected his right hand and took the violin from him for many years. Nevertheless, the great musician was able to overcome the disease and return to the stage. His right arm was still affected, and when he moved the bow upward, his hand shook; he had to fight it all the time. Still there was an indescribable aura around him; something hypnotic was in his sound, something that we had never heard before from any Russian violinist.

11 · Military Ensemble: Private Mikhail

All men in the USSR must serve in the army, unless one had a good excuse not to. I did not have one, and was ready to do my duty after college graduation. Men with college degrees served 12 months in the army; those without were required to serve 18 months. Just a few weeks before my graduation, the government changed this rule. Now men with college degrees had to serve 18 months, and those without, 24 months. Despite this hit, I was fortunate enough to be accepted into the Song and Dance Ensemble of the Moscow Military District, where the small orchestra played marches, sang patriotic folk songs, and accompanied dancers. No, I did not dance, but I did have the opportunity to test my voice on a few occasions. My career as a singer did not advance any further and I happily returned to my fiddle. I never touched a gun and served all 18 months playing music. As part of the ensemble routine, once a week I scrubbed the hardwood floors in the long, wide corridor of our barracks with a piece of glass so that they could be polished afterwards. Of course, we cut our hands all the time. A few times I was punished for not being a very good soldier, and was sent to clean up the toilets (yes, with my bare hands).

In my military uniform

The Artistic Director of the ensemble was a colonel. His name was Suren Babloev. He would come to our barracks, usually drunk (he favored Armenian Cognac), and create an atmosphere of anxiety and fear among the personnel. We never knew what to expect from him but were aware that his power over our lives was almost absolute. He was like thunder and lightning, and in the blink of an eye, he could change a soldier's life forever, which happened once in my presence. On this occasion, he got angry with one of the soldiers, a pianist, and ordered him to be transferred out of the ensemble and into the tank division. This was essentially a death sentence on the poor man. He probably ruined his hands and lost his future career as a pianist. We never heard from him again. Though Babloev himself conducted our dress rehearsals and concerts, all of the preparation was done by his assistants who held rehearsals daily and also wrote numerous arrangements, though these were always credited to Babloev.

Babloev also made a habit of singling out some fortunate individuals and making their lives as amazing as he made others' miserable. For unknown reasons, Babloev liked Viktor, one of the soldiers, enough to make him his personal adjutant. Viktor was no longer obligated to follow the strict rules that applied to the rest of the ensemble. Even the two other officers of the ensemble, the Captain and Sergeant, had no power over Viktor, and even tried to win his friendship, knowing that Victor had influence over Babloev. Viktor became Babloev's personal driver and lived with an open schedule. He was a free man dressed in a military uniform. Fortunately for me, I was friends with Viktor, and sometimes had access to the "chief's" room, once even having the privilege of sitting in Babloev's leather armchair in the colonel's absence.

The next officer in rank was Captain (his name escapes me). He was in charge of the ideological life of the ensemble. His job was primarily to hold daily meetings with soldiers and conduct reports on the political life of the USSR and other socialist countries and their enemies. These sessions were the most boring part of our days. The Captain had an extremely poor vocabulary and an evidently low IQ, and everyone in the ensemble made fun of him.

The real person who controlled the life of the ensemble was Sergeant Piotr Shaboltai. There were 50 soldiers in the ensemble including instrumental players, singers, and dancers. The Sergeant knew everything about everybody. He was a natural manipulator. Like an actor on a stage, he desperately needed an audience, and who could be a better audience than a few dozen obedient and powerless soldiers? Every morning at exactly 7:00 a.m., he would enter the common room in which we slept. Switching on the lights, he would yell, "*Pod'em* (rise) in 45 seconds!" This meant that all the soldiers had to wake up, get up, get fully dressed, run into the main lobby, and line up in special order, all within 45 seconds. We had to make sure that every button on our uniforms was buttoned and that our belts were tightly fastened. Then, with an evil smirk on his face, Shaboltai would check every soldier's uniform; if he found that someone's belt was a bit too loose, or that the belt buckle wasn't shiny enough, he would scream, "*Otboi!* (retreat) in 45 seconds!" and everything would rewind just like in a movie. We would run like crazy back to our room, undress, place our perfectly folded uniform on the stool next to our beds, and climb back under the covers. Then followed 45 seconds of "Rise!" again, and the nightmare would start over. Shaboltai would do it as many times as he felt was necessary to satisfy his boredom (and to demonstrate his power). After the "final" lineup, he would demand we take off our uniform tops and go for a two-mile run outside in the frozen winter air. This would finally wake us up and invigorate our hunger, making us ready for breakfast. Breakfast every day was the same: porridge from unidentifiable ingredients. There was a rampant rumor that the army officials added bromine to the food in order to lower the soldiers' libidos, but seeing as we did not have any other food choices, we gradually grew accustomed to the gruel.

Russian Military Ensemble. I am in the center, right behind the music stand.

In the barracks next to ours, there was a military company of about 250 people who were specially trained to march in ceremonial processions in Red Square in front of Lenin's Mausoleum. All of these soldiers were at least six feet tall, and their entire days were spent practicing their specially choreographed routine. They moved majestically. The soldiers spent the rest of their time working out and, due to their discipline, had tremendous endurance. Perhaps because of the endless monotony of their lives, at times brutal violence would erupt within the group. It wasn't a wonder; these young, strong men had to spend two years far away from their families and any women, with only their monotonous exercises as company. Fortunately for us, we practically never had contact with these "marching machines," only occasionally dining in the same common area.

Interlude

I was twenty in 1975 and worshipped the Beatles, Hemingway, and Modigliani. Though I have not yet composed a good song and consider myself a total failure as a painter, I did write a number of poems and essays in my twenties, all in Russian. Some of them are not so bad, and it's a pity that their beauty will most likely be lost in translation. Nevertheless, I am taking a deep breath, and with courage and a small increase in heart rate, I would like to offer you a lyrical sketch about the city where I was born.

The Heat[4]

The heat raged as if it wanted to suffocate everybody. There was no escaping the stranglehold of its monstrous fire-tipped claws.
We fought it as best we could. At sunrise windows and doors got closed and draped. We sat down in armchairs, facing laboring fans, and sinking in their stickiness, watched the evening.
A sharp telephone ring would pierce the padded twilight, and a voice decomposed by the heat sounded in the receiver.
Nothing helped, and when the temperature outside reached that in the room, windows were opened wide so the stifling dark indoor air yielded to the blazing sun.
Outside it was impossible to take a deep breath; as in a Russian bath, the air singed your nostrils and lungs.
Days seemed endless. It was a day-by-day struggle for survival while at night you'd toss on sweat-soaked sheets, hopelessly fleeing dream killers.
It was only mid-July. It was frightening to even think of August: of grass bleached white, shriveled leaves, drought-cracked dirt, and molten asphalt.
Ah, it was a glorious time!

1975

---

4 Translated by Nikolai Popov, 2015

12 · My First Marriage

My friendship with Alla began during our first year of college. It survived the volatility of youth and slowly transformed into a deeper passion. When people are in love, they often start writing poetry. I was not an exception. Though I did not rise to the level of Pushkin, a few of my poems still make my heart beat a bit faster, and I have to say there is some music to them.

We got married while I was still serving in the Soviet Army. I got two days off for the occasion. The wedding took place in a fancy restaurant called Praga that was located in Arbat, an old neighborhood in Moscow. The festivities took place in a large room appropriately called the "Winter Garden," which was decorated with real flowers and trees. Many friends and relatives, mostly from the bride's side, attended the wedding. The food was delicious: hot and cold smoked fish, European sausages, beef tongue with horseradish, red and black caviar, other delicacies, and a whole lot of champagne. The wedding was wonderful, but soon its intoxicating flavor went away and life returned to its everyday course.

Moscow had always had a housing problem. Even my father-in-law's connections in the distribution world (he was the associate director of a large construction company) were not enough to get the newlyweds a place of their own. My in-laws, wife, and I got stuck in a small one-bedroom apartment on the fourth floor of a five-story building with no elevator. The in-laws took the bedroom. To get to the bathroom they had to go through the living room where Alla and I slept on a foldout sofa. In spite of the less-than-ideal setup we were lucky to have a flat in a good neighborhood, only a fifteen minute walk from the subway station.

The real complications started a year later with the birth of our adorable baby Yulia. She was a light sleeper, and would wake frequently during the night with the subtlest of noises. Once awake, she would cry out in hunger, waking everyone else in the household as well. This went on for months. In the morning my father-in-law would go to work, and Alla and I to our rehearsals. Needless to say, on more than one occasion I almost fell asleep and dropped my violin during my morning rehearsals, and I was sure my wife was in the same predicament. My mother-in-law stayed at home and took care of the baby, the cleaning, and cooking (I can still taste her delicious poppy seed pie). She had never worked, for her husband was a good provider, and she had chronic health issues. Unfortunately, she used her migraines and high blood pressure as a tool to control the family and dictate her rules, and nobody dared to argue with a woman in fragile health. The apartment was her kingdom and even an accidental deviation from her rules triggered a war in the family. In exchange for her work at home she demanded total obedience.

Her husband was fifteen years older than she was, and loved her deeply, having surrendered many years ago to her strong will. In contrast, Alla had a peaceful character and always tried to avoid conflict. Having grown up in a provincial town, I came from a simple family and had to learn many things that were standard in their family. I didn't even know how to properly use a fork and knife at the table. I caught on quickly to table manners, but refused to follow my mother-in-law's orders. Twenty months of subordination in the Soviet Army was enough for me.

My wife went back to work soon after her maternity leave was over. Each night around midnight when the evening shows ended, I would meet her at the subway station and we would walk home together.

Due to the constant stress at home, our patience began to wear thin over time and our relationship grew very tense. We were all just exhausted, both physically and emotionally. Alla tried not to take sides, but at a certain point this became impossible. There was no solution, and I knew if things continued as they were, my spirit would be broken. I suffered terribly; I loved Alla and our baby, but it had come to the point where we could no longer coexist. Our marriage came to an end, and the divorce left a permanent scar on me.

My ex-father-in-law passed away twenty-five years ago, and Alla, who had been healthy her entire life, died under mysterious circumstances at the age of fifty-two. Ironically my ex-mother-in-law is still around, turning ninety as I write. She has managed to outlive her entire family.

13 · The Bolshoi Theatre

At the time we were married, Alla was already working in the Symphony Orchestra of the Bolshoi Theatre. She was an extremely hard worker, and her family was very proud of her success. The Symphony Orchestra of the Bolshoi was in the highest paid category of all the orchestras in Moscow, and effectively the entire USSR. Only two other orchestras paid as well: the State Symphony Orchestra and the Symphony Orchestra of Radio and Television. In these orchestras, section musicians were paid 220 rubles a month, and the concertmaster's salary was as high as 500 rubles. The workload at the Bolshoi Orchestra was huge, though fortunately there was a limit on the number of shows per month. Musicians were to play no more than twenty-seven shows a month (including operas and ballets) plus attend an unlimited amount of the rehearsals with one day off a week. A typical workday looked like this: a morning rehearsal for three to four hours, lunch at home, practice for a couple of hours, maybe take a short nap, and a performance at night. The repertoire was heavy with Russian operas and many of them were very long, often spanning four hours. Barely making it home before midnight, one had to be ready the next day for morning rehearsal.

Every new production of an opera had unlimited rehearsals. For example, Glinka's opera *Ivan Susanin* had over 100 rehearsals! The same was true of Wagner's *Das Rheingold*. By the first performance all the musicians knew their orchestral parts by heart. The operas and ballets were different every night, never two of the same in a row, and everyone had to be on their toes. Because it was the best job in the city (and also because it simply wasn't the way), nobody complained.

The orchestra consisted of 270 musicians. There were, in effect, three full rotating orchestras, enough musicians to sustain the whirlpool of shows. The trouble began when the orchestra started to tour abroad. Only 90 of the 270 musicians could tour, which caused all sorts of hell to break loose. In addition to the special KGB department at the theatre, which screened every musician at least three generations back, the musicians themselves began to scheme against one another in hopes of being chosen as a touring member. They would compose anonymous letters about each other, stating how their colleagues planned to defect on tour. Suddenly the KGB department had a lot to do! Not many knew that the Bolshoi Theatre was financed by the USSR Ministry of Defense. Because of this, there was never a shortage of financial support, but every coin has two sides. The touring roster changed every day, and only the most "trusted" were allowed to represent this top Soviet cultural institution abroad.

Alla was lucky enough to be one of the touring musicians on a few occasions. One time there was a tragic accident involving one of the musicians. The orchestra was touring by bus in Greece, crossing the mountains. As the buses were not equipped with toilets, every couple of hours they would stop alongside the cliffs and women would go 'to the right' while men would go 'to the left.' One of the male musicians came too close to the cliff's edge, slipped and fell. There was no help around and no cell phones yet.

One of the conductors, Fuat Mansurov was also traveling on the bus. He was a skilled mountain climber. The Bolshoi Theatre people used to tease him by calling him "the best climber among the conductors, and the best conductor among the climbers." Somebody found a rope, and Mansurov was able to use it to climb down, only to find that the poor musician had fallen to his death.

I, too, had the honor of being part of the Bolshoi Orchestra for a short period of time after playing a successful audition. I was nervous coming to my first rehearsal. Before entering the orchestra pit, musicians always looked at the orchestra roster listings to find out what their next show would be. I was so proud to see my name on that list, but my pride did not last long. By the end of the first week of rehearsals, I could no longer find my name on the roster. I could see the place where my name had been, and it had been erased. I rushed to the manager to ask what was going on and learned that my services were "no longer needed." No other explanation was offered. That was the end of my Bolshoi career, and I had to look for another job.

In those days, Jews were limited as to what jobs they could get and even what colleges they could attend. Anti-Semitism was always on the government's unspoken agenda. The hatred of Jews was like a cancer that had started spreading throughout society many centuries prior, reaching its peak during the time of socialism.

Most colleges had a quota on Jews, which meant that because Jews made up three percent of the population of the Soviet Union, their admittance to colleges and universities was also limited to three percent of the total student body.

Perhaps owing to the initiative of their directors, both the Moscow Conservatory and Gnessin Musical College were exceptions to this rule. Everybody knew about the quotas, and all musicians knew that Jews could never get a job with the Radio and Television Symphony Orchestra. The man who was at the time the Minister of Russian Media (aka propaganda) made himself very clear: as long as he remained in his position, not a single Jew would get a job in that orchestra. How much more transparent could he be? I decided it wasn't even worth trying; the application would be returned with some ridiculous explanation, and I would never have the chance to audition. Why waste the distinguished audition committee's valuable time?

14 · Moscow State Symphony Orchestra

In Russia there was never a shortage of Jewish musicians, especially string players. We were fortunate that during that time of
intense anti-Semitism, Veronica Dudarova, Music Director of the
Moscow State Symphony Orchestra, was not afraid to give us jobs.
I played an audition, she liked me, and I became a member of the
first violin section. Very soon there was an opening for the Assistant Principal Second Violin position, and I auditioned again. I
got the job, and spent the next ten years holding that position.

The building in which we rehearsed used to be a church 60
years back. After religion was banned from society under the socialist regime, many churches in Russia became inactive or were destroyed. This building survived and was given to our orchestra by
the state. It became our permanent home, a welcome change from
our constantly changing rehearsal spaces.

The church was not big, but it accommodated about 90 musicians, a music library, and offices for the conductor and director.
During its remodeling, the church was restructured into two stories.
The second floor became our cozy café where we could buy snacks,
tea, or coffee. There was actually a person making sandwiches while
we practiced, and during our 10-minute breaks we would rush to
buy the sandwiches before they sold out. We musicians tended to
build up quite the appetite while we worked.

There was no air conditioning in the rehearsal space, just two
small windows used for ventilation (called *fortochka*) on opposite
sides of the room: one behind the cellos and double basses, and another behind the violins. Both windows were kept tightly sealed
during long rehearsal hours, especially during the cold Moscow
winters, and would rarely be opened during breaks. If open, the
winter air would rush into the room, creating a danger for string
instruments, and wreaking havoc on the tuning of the woodwinds,
both being especially sensitive to fluctuations in temperature. It was
so stuffy in the room that we used a famous Russian expression ("to
hang an ax in the air") to describe the thickness of the stale air.

In the very back of the large room was a small foyer leading
to the bathrooms. This foyer experienced heavy traffic from the
smokers during every break (comprised of at least half of the or-

chestra). During the break, these foyer doors would open every other second, and the cigarette smoke would inevitably enter the rehearsal room. After rehearsal, all of our clothes, including our coats that we kept on our chairs because there was no cloak room, reeked of cigarettes.

Dudarova was a unique character; we called her *"tipazh"* (Russian slang for some combination of unpredictability, ego, and artistry). Firstly, she could not conduct at all. Her "technique" included rotating her shoulders in unpredictable directions and circling her wrists in an odd manner. The musicians had to decode these gestures, and we tried our best, but her convulsions created a very different response in different musicians. The beat was so unclear that it created chaos in the orchestra. Naturally, she would get upset, blaming the orchestra for not being able to play together. Our rehearsals went on for hours and hours.

We would come in at 10 a.m. for a standard four-hour rehearsal, and around 1:30 p.m. she would scream, "You are a lousy orchestra! You cannot play together! We need more time to rehearse." A break would be announced, and the rehearsal would resume at 3 p.m. for another two hours. Though she was a terrible conductor, she had a huge heart. When she conducted, she was truly in the music, and we knew that her emotions were genuine. I recall a couple of remarkable and quite extravagant episodes from our concerts that I would like to share with you.

The orchestra was often chosen to play at funeral services. It was quite an honor for the group to play heart-wrenching music when our top party leaders went to a better place. We played at the funerals of Brezhnev, Kosygin, Andropov, and other "great" Russian leaders. At one point it seemed they were dying one right after another. The services were always held at the Kolonnyi (Pillar) Hall of the House of the Unions. It's a beautiful building with excellent acoustics. The hall was named after a series of round wooden columns covered with white marble, which along with a few rows of crystal chandeliers created a festive atmosphere. The hall was built at the end of the 18th century and was used for classical music concerts. After the 1917 revolution, the Russian government assigned it to the Trade of Unions and it was often used for funeral services.

It was November, 1982. Winter came early that year, but all the doors were wide open and people kept coming in, waiting in long lines to pay their final tribute to their "beloved" leader, Leonid Brezhnev. We were dressed very formally: tails for the men and long black dresses for the women, so we put on a lot of warm clothes underneath our formal wear. We all looked like puffy bears. I clearly remember what we played that time: J. S. Bach's *Prelude and Fugue in D minor,* transcribed for the orchestra. This magnificent piece made people cry, especially on such an occasion.

The orchestra approached the climax of the piece, roaring like an organ. Here came the final chord, powerful enough to raise the dead, not that it was anybody's intention to do so. We finished the last chord and the music stopped, but the conductor did not. Dudarova was so carried away by the music that she could not stop conducting. She continued to wave her hands in total silence. All the musicians stared at her in disbelief. None of us had ever seen anything like this before. It was like watching a silent movie. Such a comical situation in a tragic atmosphere was far beyond Kafka's imagination. I felt an enormous spasm of laughter erupting from my chest. I was so afraid to burst out laughing that I put my head between my knees. My body was convulsing in spasms. I felt tears pouring out of my eyes, leaving a trail of drops between my feet. I'll bet I was not alone, though some people might have read my tears as a reaction to the funeral. The worst part was that all such events were recorded for later TV news. A break followed and Dudarova asked her assistant to come to her room. "What happened, Kostya?" she asked. "What happened?" he repeated like a parrot. "Did you notice anything?" "No, I did not notice anything." "*Horosho*" ("Very well"), she said, and let him go. The same night this recording was demagnetized and never went public.

I was lucky to become close friends with Kostya, a brilliant violinist and conductor. We spent many evenings in his tiny kitchen after rehearsals, trying to solve all the problems of our society. These meetings were always accompanied by vodka and anecdotes. By the 1980s it was slowly becoming less dangerous to tell political jokes among friends. Thirty or forty years prior one would definitely end up in prison for that. The most popular political anecdote at the time was one that we called "first prize or 25 years in prison." It goes like this: Two worms, a father and son, sit in a huge steaming pile of shit, enjoying its warmth and comfort. The son suddenly sticks his head out of the pile and asks, "Dad, look there is sun out there and fresh air. Why are we sitting in here?" His father replied, "This is our homeland, son."

Every summer the orchestra went on tour locally, which all of the musicians, especially the men, liked a lot. Are you curious as to why this was the case? Read on.

Each year we alternated between two cities, Sochi and Kislovodsk. Sochi is now internationally known because it hosted the XXII Olympic Winter Games in 2014. It has beautiful architecture and has always been a resort destination for Russians as well as foreign tourists. Its main attraction is the warm water of the Black Sea. Summers there were not too hot and the humidity was low. Hundreds of people arrived every day to the city, and rushed straight to the beach. We were no exception, spending most of our free time on the beach, and playing evening concerts when the air had cooled down. The men from the orchestra (not all, but a majority) would change mysteriously from the moment they step out of the plane. They were on the hunt. I was always amazed by the sudden change in their behavior, since most of the men were married. By the time of our first concert, usually on the day of our arrival, the "luckiest" hunters were already bringing their new mistresses to the concert. During our 30 day stopovers in Sochi I saw quite a lot of turnover among their new "friends."

Kislovodsk was also a beautiful resort, famous for having the biggest city park in Europe and the healing *narzan* baths. Our time spent there did not reflect much of a change in terms of the musicians' behavior, except that the search was not so easy. People coming there had more physical problems than those in Sochi, and were not as likely to fall into quick affairs.

My position with this orchestra was my first full-time job. I was 25 and still boiling over with ideas of how things should be, impressions carried over from my college days. Inevitably, these ideals clashed violently with the realities of orchestral life. The striking unprofessionalism of our conductor, her meaningless diatribes, and torturous rehearsals drove all of the musicians crazy, and everybody had to cope with the situation in his or her own way. Leaving rehearsals, I was often annoyed and sometimes even furious. I could not stop complaining and my most frequent lament was, "Why should it be this way?" One of my friends and colleagues, cellist Grisha Katz, who had already been with the orchestra for a few years, imparted some words of wisdom: "Misha, the rehearsal is over. The doors have shut behind you; now it's time to erase it from your memory and let it go." I found this difficult advice to follow, but it was the only sane way to survive the sheer ridiculousness of those days. Any individual expression of dissatisfaction would result in immediate job loss, but the time of unifying the entire orchestra into one fiery fist of protest was slowly growing nearer. That day would not come for another ten years.

15 · Tours Abroad

I traveled a lot with the Moscow State Symphony. Our European tours included Bulgaria, the Czech Republic, Slovakia, and Yugoslavia. When we visited Poland, I learned that Polish people called their capital, Warsaw, "Little Paris," though we did not see any resemblance. (When I visited Paris I certainly never heard the French call it "Big Warsaw.") A visit to Turkey reminded me of my native Kyrgyzstan. Three month-long South American tours brought us to Venezuela, Mexico, Argentina, Brazil, Uruguay, Panama, and Colombia. Russian musicians were super cheap to hire. We did not get paid extra for tours abroad, but received so called "per diem." Per diem was supposed to be used for basic needs, mostly food, and was around 10 US dollars per day. None of the Russian musicians ever used this money for basic needs, but saved it to buy things they could resell back in Russia for a profit. Since there was a shortage of everything in our native land in those days, making a profit was very easy, but to make a good profit one needed to be a real "artist." We learned the fundamentals of capitalism right there on the spot. It is ironic that the Soviet system actually provoked its people to explore the taste of free enterprise.

But how did we eat during that long month of travel? Each musician brought along a big suitcase filled with an amazing variety of non-perishable food. The suitcases were really heavy. Do you remember that blessed time when the airlines were not in crisis and passengers were allowed to take just about anything they could carry onboard? Since we traveled on Aeroflot charter flights, we never had problems with luggage weight restrictions. (On a side note, a funny anecdote just came to mind. A Russian *reclama* (advertisement) insists, "Fly with Aeroflot planes, there are only a few left!")

We called this special suitcase our "*chemodan-restoran*" (suitcase-restaurant). As you can see, these two words rhyme in Russian and there is some poetry to it. Some food needed to be prepared, so someone brought a portable stove. Want fresh tea? No problem: you could boil the water in the glass with a small boiler, but most such commercial boilers took too long to boil a cup of water. This is where the genius Russian mind, famous for exploration and discovery, stepped in to create self-made boilers. Please sit tight, since I am going to give away our top secret of how you, too, can make your own hot water boiler. It might come in handy in case you hate your microwave, but want a cup of boiling water within seconds.

First you have to find two old-fashioned razor blades, used for shaving between the 1930s and 1950s. Used blades are OK, but it's better if they're new as they work faster. Take two wires to make plus and minus (positive and negative) and connect them to the blades. The blades should never touch each other. (You know what happens if they connect? If you don't, then you most likely got a "D" in physics.) Make a plug on the other side and stick it in the outlet, but let me warn you: these two blades make water boil in seconds not because it's a Russian miracle, but because they are very thin, and the electricity runs very quickly between them. This makes them powerful and takes a lot of energy. Most likely nothing will happen with your fuses at home; just ask other family members not to try it simultaneously.

Five minutes after our orchestra checked in at the hotel, the power went out. I don't need to mention that this happened in every hotel we visited. I am sure that the local people learned their lesson, and next time before inviting Russians they made sure to update their electrical system.

What could be tastier than crackers with canned sardines or chicken noodle soup from a package? Forget that it expired a long time ago, since it was bought in bulk in preparation for a tour that might or might not happen in the future. Many times we witnessed staples such as salt or matches disappearing from our shops overnight with no promise of return. For that reason, everybody kept an "extra" 10-20 kilograms of salt or 100 boxes of matches; in other words, anything nonperishable. Foreign tourists who were invited to a friend's house were always amazed; there was an abundance of food on the table and the fridges were full, but the store shelves were empty. It was the exact opposite of what they had in their countries. We had to buy those soup packages whenever they were available, since they could disappear from the store as unexpectedly as they appeared.

The concert schedule was intense. We often played concerts every day in a different city, and also had rehearsals or a sound check prior to the concert. We still managed to find the time to conduct "artistic" business (see above), and also find some entertainment. Though it might sound embarrassing now, I have to tell you about an extremely exciting experience the Russian musicians had on a tour. Since this book might accidently end up in the hands of an eight-year-old, I will be brief.

On our first trip to Latin America, our first stop was Venezuela. As we landed at Caracas International Airport we received great news: overnight, the bolivar had dropped 100% compared to the US dollar (and we were paid in dollars). This news filled our musician hearts with happiness. Did we care that the local economy was in deep trouble? Not at all. We had a different mission on tour, and so far it was starting out nicely for us. That first day we had a few hours free, and after checking in at the hotel we decided not to ruin its electrical system right away; we were still full from the food provided on the plane. (Without criticizing today's travel, I have to tell our kids and grandkids the truth that in the old days there was real food on planes regardless of the length of the flight, and it was great food! I clearly remember caviar served with unlimited drinks on international flights for no charge. I am sorry about what you have to eat today on flights. Anyway, you get the picture.)

It was hard to cross the streets, since the traffic never stopped. It

On tour with Moscow State Symphony in Venezuela

seemed that there were no traffic lights, or maybe we were trying to cross a highway. Russia did not have highways, and we expected traffic to stop at some point. We ignored the signs for overpasses, or any other signs in general, just because Russians don't ever follow the signs, and also because nobody could read Spanish. Even if we had wanted to follow the signs, we were completely unfamiliar with road signs since most Russians didn't own cars. We were en route to an "adult" cinema, something we couldn't do back in the USSR, and we were determined.

In Caracas we learned about children's organized crime. On the first day a couple of women from the orchestra got their purses stolen and silver necklaces ripped off their necks while on a walk. It was impossible to catch the young criminals, who ran like rats and knew every little place to hide. I did not like Uruguay at all. On the street somebody snapped the watch from my wrist. No big deal, at least nobody stuck a knife between my ribs, but the watch had been a gift. My girlfriend Larisa, who would soon become my wife, had given me that beautiful Seiko watch so I could set an alarm and not be late for the bus. Of course, there were watches in Russia, but none of them had alarms. The flexible plastic wristband easily snapped off my wrist, and I hardly felt it happen. I have to tell you, the guy who did it was a virtuoso. Despite the loss, I have some respect for his skills. On my return to Moscow the disappearance of the watch did not go unnoticed, but the bitterness of the event was quickly erased when I showed Larisa the gifts I had acquired abroad.

Colombia impressed me with its enormous silver business as well as its bloody violence. In Bogota we heard a few explosions, and saw people running in panic. Local drug cartels were fighting for territory, but who could stop Russian musicians on the hunt for bargains? Once, when I was in my hotel room and ready to depart for rehearsal, I heard shots fired, and jumped to the window. I saw a man running and a few police officers following him. The man was limping. It seemed that he was injured. Then the man fell on his knees and the police surrounded him. What followed after still stands before my eyes. One of the policemen approached the man from behind and shot him in the back of the head.

Buenos Aires was much more peaceful, and full of Museums of

Meat. That is what they called the meat stores. They were impressive, though we could not comprehend how anybody could find anything in that store with literally hundreds and hundreds of different types of meat and sausages. I am sure they now use computers with special software to locate something that customers want to find. I have to mention that we unanimously ignored those museums.

Brazil was different. First of all, our hotel was right on the beach, and for the first time we saw what later would become standard women's beach wear: thongs. We had never seen them before and after seeing so many beautiful women we foolishly imagined they were all single. Ah well, we could dream. Outfitted in our Soviet swimming trousers, we must have made a strong, possibly unforgettable, impression on those ladies. I can still hear them crying for us. Don't cry for me, Brasilia!

Barcelona was a beauty. Its long, straight avenues filled me with a feeling of order and tradition. Everywhere we played the audiences were ecstatic. We played with passion. People always felt that there was sincere feeling in the music, not just polished precision. We were generous with our playing, and a few encores followed the main program, always bringing even bigger storms of applause. In response, the local people were generous with the parties after the concerts, and in each country we learned something new about its cuisine. It was hard to return to our *chemodan-restoran* after such parties.

Traditionally, we took a lot of Russian music on tour. After all, it wasn't surprising that audiences abroad wanted to hear a Russian orchestra perform Russian music. This tradition is still popular around the world when it comes to a touring symphony orchestra. One night we were scheduled to play Tchaikovsky's Symphony No. 5. That night Dudarova came on stage, bowed to the audience, turned to the orchestra, and without opening the score raised her hands in an energetic gesture. She never conducted from memory, but her gesture was an unmistakable invitation to start Tchaikovsky's Symphony No. 4 with its famous loud trumpet call. The trumpeters did not even raise their instruments. Her hands froze in the air. She noticed that something was terribly wrong. Hands still above her head, she bent down to the first stand of violas and asked in a quiet voice, "What symphony are we playing tonight?" "No. 5," responded the principal violist. (No. 5 starts very quietly with strings and clarinets only.) She slowly lowered her hands and gave the proper gesture to the strings. The music started. As usual, a grateful audience gave us a standing ovation, and asked the conductor to return three times for a bow.

One more case shows how much Dudarova was not in her right mind. She always took with her on tour a woman who took care of her clothing. That night Dudarova was in so much of a hurry that she put on two different shoes and went like that on stage. Not only were the shoes different, but the heels were of different heights! The difference was not dramatic, but it was enough for us to notice her slight limp as she walked to the podium. She seemed not to notice anything and conducted the concert with great passion.

No one in a Soviet orchestra could go on a foreign tour without a special KGB officer assigned to go with the group. The point was to watch the musicians to make sure no one would defect. Everybody knew this, including the foreign company that hosted the orchestra. But in order to keep up the façade, this officer was included in the orchestra roster, usually as a fourth bassoon. The musicians understood how ridiculous it was to have four bassoon players in the orchestra, but everybody just ignored it; this fourth wheel was part of a non-negotiable package deal. We usually would not see this person around, since he was busy with standard spy business, and rarely had time to actually watch us.

16 · Quartet

One day I got a call from a man I did not know well. He was one of the concertmasters of the Bolshoi Theatre Orchestra, and I had met him a few times when I worked there. Evidently he remembered me. Sergei Ryabov asked if I would be interested in playing in the String Quartet of the Union of Composers of the USSR, where he played first violin. It was very tempting, since it would be a good opportunity to play string quartets in the company of strong musicians, an experience I missed since college graduation. I agreed, and it became my part-time job in addition to a full-time job with the Moscow State Symphony.

Ryabov was not an easy man to work with, but he liked me, and that made the time we spent together almost fun. Half the music we played was classical repertoire and the other half was by contemporary Soviet composers, who were members of the Union of Composers. It was a big deal to be a member of this club. Once a young composer was inducted, his music would be played by orchestras and chamber groups. We often premiered the new pieces; some were even dedicated to us. But the most remarkable opportunity that came along was a tour that presented new Soviet music to audiences abroad. First, we took two local tours to present the new composition of a Turkmenian composer Chari Nurimov. It was a String Quartet written in memory of the great Indian leader, Jawaharlal Nehru. Russia and India were very close at that time. The music of the quartet was supposed to be based on Indian folk motifs, and we learned new techniques such as quarter step tones, slow glissandos, and other tricks. Obviously nobody from our Soviet audiences could tell whether it actually sounded like Indian music. Ryabov, being a strategist, planned to present the music in India, but first we traveled to Kazakhstan to test the quality of our new string quartet.

The concerts we played in Kazakhstan took place mostly at *kolhoz* (community farms) and were tremendously successful. We would start the concert with some Beethoven, then play Nurimov's quartet (fortunately it was short), and end with Brahms' *Hungarian Dances* or other brilliant encores. It's very hard to describe those audiences. It is likely that those people had never in their lives heard of a string quartet. They worked very hard all their lives on their farms, their faces were burned by the merciless sun, and they bathed in the river.

It was a rule that the chairman of the *kolhoz* was present at the concert, and he would take us to the party after the concert. The parties were unforgettable. A sheep was slaughtered for the occasion, and as VIPs from the heart of Russia, we were given the privilege of tasting the sheep's eyes and ears. Endless bottles of vodka helped us digest the fatty meats and heaping plates of *plov* (pilaf). We stayed in yurts. The biggest challenge was to find a place to use the restroom at night somewhere in total darkness. The pale moon shone between the clouds, laughing at us.

The second tour took us to the Russian Far East. After an almost ten-hour flight, we landed in Vladivostok. We were well prepared for that voyage. Our agent who organized the tour had informed us of the unofficial "dry law" in the region. The whole economy of the region was based on fishing for salmon, beluga, and other expensive fish. Once a year, for a very short period of time, all of the people were busy catching fish ripe with caviar. They call it "caviar season." At this time the selling of any alcohol was absolutely prohibited. (When fishing season was over, everyone would go back to their heavy drinking, since there were no other jobs available.) This did not mean that people stopped producing their own homemade alcohol, but rather that the quality of non-commercial products was not high.

We were advised to take with us Stolichnaya vodka and Armenian cognac, as much as we could fit in our suitcases. I bet you can already guess that we didn't take it along for our own consumption. Once more we proved that the socialist economic system could live very well alongside the oldest principle of the economy: a simple exchange of goods. Our exchange business worked very well: for one bottle of vodka we could receive up to three liters of red caviar of unparalleled quality. The most successful exchange, however, took place when a half liter bottle of Armenian cognac was exchanged for one liter of black caviar. I dare not imagine our cholesterol levels following that feast.

The climax of our existence as a distinguished quartet was our one-month tour in India. Upon our arrival in Delhi, the very first thing that struck my eyes and my heart was the sight of crippled children. They were everywhere – on each plaza and every street corner. We learned that over 80% of the Indian population lived in horrible poverty. It was impossible for most people to get an education or job. We were told that "merciful" parents would break their children's limbs so that when they grew, their limbs would grow in the wrong direction. When tourists saw them they would be so horrified that they would give some change to the children. To these families, the only other option was starvation. The cellist from our quartet who had first visited India ten years earlier swore that she recognized the same crippled boy, now a young man, sitting on the same street corner.

Apart from the unbelievable poverty, India impressed us with its ancient history and the architectural beauty of its palaces. Our visit to India was part of a governmental cultural exchange. First class hotels were provided for our stay. Since there was a lot of disagreement at that time between the political parties, violence was a possibility, and we were heavily guarded. In the hotels we always had an armed guard next to each of our rooms day and night. Our big concert in Delhi was organized with a lot of security. The brother of India's President Indira Gandhi was present at our concert. We performed the famous quartet by Nurimov, and people cried. Our success was overwhelming.

When I came to India I did not know that it had become home to an outstanding Russian painter, Svetoslav Roerich, son of the famous painter Nicholas Roerich. Our agent organized a meeting at his house, and it was very inspiring to be in the presence of a living legend who walked us through his home gallery. Before we said goodbye, Roerich handed me a note with beautiful Indian sculptures on which he had written (in Russian), "Let's always aspire towards excellence."

As part of our itinerary we played one concert in Sri Lanka (formerly Ceylon). The next day after the concert we went sightseeing and got caught in a very unpleasant situation. We were walking along the street when shots were fired. People around us started to scream and run, but nobody knew where the shots had come from, so everybody was panicking, creating even more chaos. In

*In India with Russian-Indian painter Svetoslav Roerich (second on the
right) and members of Union of Composers String Quartet*

the midst of this we completely forgot where our hotel was. Finally,
somebody pointed us in the right direction, and we ran toward the
hotel. It seemed that our security guards were more scared for us
than we were for ourselves, and they were very happy to see us return unharmed.

During the tour we ate at the hotel three times a day, enjoying
excellent food. Because tourists often got sick in India due to the
water, we were warned to be extremely careful in this regard long
before our trip. Even with Russia's low quality of drinking water
and our strong stomachs, there was still cause for concern. We were
very careful and never drank any water except in the hotel, which
was supposed to have a special water purifying system. Our month
in India was coming to a close, and we just had to play our final
concert in the evening. The return flight was scheduled for the next
morning.

We had a tasty lunch at the hotel, and when the waiter brought
us water, I remember asking him if it was purified. He nodded his
head. (Only later, when I started my investigation, did I learn that
most of the waiters didn't speak English well, and they were told
simply to agree to all questions they were asked by nodding their
head.) A couple of hours later my colleagues and I felt that some-

thing in our stomachs was moving much faster than we expected, which prompted a competition of who would get to the bathroom first. It was ruthless; we had no mercy for one other. No one really knows how we managed to stay onstage for the duration of that final concert. I do recall worrying that the sounds from our guts would overpower the softer passages in our performance.

Just a little over a month after our return to Moscow from the Indian trip, I was scheduled to go on a trip with the Moscow State Symphony. However, since returning home, I was feeling worse and worse every day. I couldn't keep any food down and was losing weight like crazy. I felt terrible; my face slowly turned pale at first and then green. I took all my prescribed antibiotics, but nothing seemed to help. That Indian bug appeared to be a very special one, and I feared I was dying. In the month since our return from India I had lost over 30 pounds. I needed all new clothes, but could not leave my house because I was so weak. Soon the only clothes I would need would be a black suit, I thought. There was no hope left and the doctors gave up on me. I clearly remember the 30th day after my return to Moscow: I woke up on that day feeling different from all the days before. My stomach was quiet, the air had a different smell, and the sun was a little brighter. The nightmare was over, and I quickly recovered my strength and was able to go on tour with the orchestra.

Our tour to Italy a year later was very different from the Indian tour. This time we brought with us a mixed program of classical and modern Russian music. The reception was overwhelming. After each concert the audience gave us a standing ovation. We loved to play encores. It was our favorite part of the concert because we could relax a bit and give people what they wanted most: dessert in the form of brilliant little miniatures.

This time we did not worry about the safety of our drinking water. It was good, tasty, and clean. The food was superb, especially the freshly caught seafood which was cooked in front of our eyes. Prior to our trip we had thought that all Italians ate was spaghetti, and were surprised by how much variety Italian cuisine had to offer (and how tasty the local wines were!). It was springtime and the hotel we stayed in had an astonishing view of the sea, just like on the postcards. Eating breakfast on the sunny veranda made us forget why we were actually there. The waiters were so friendly and it did not feel like a business trip at all. When we walked down the street, tourists would ask me for directions. With my dark beard and light brown leather jacket, I was frequently taken for a local. We had a special tour bus, and I was amazed at the skills of our bus drivers who managed to navigate through the narrowest streets, leaving mere inches between our bus and their brick walls.

17 · The Decline of the Golden Era

In the 1970s and 1980s the Russian economy was in deep stagnation. In fact, the period from the mid-60s through the 70s was officially termed "the era of stagnation." People could not buy basic food or medical supplies. The era that followed was *glasnost* (openness, which meant a decrease in censorship and an increase in freedom of information, and *perestroika* (a restructuring of society). This was an attempt to liberalize the economy and reverse stagnation. It was not a success; major economic and social reforms were not carried out, and Russian morale was at its lowest point. People no longer believed in a "bright future," a term that was used in Russia to describe communism. According to a firm statement issued by Nikita Khrushchev, one of the progressive Russian party leaders of the time, communism was supposed to have been built in the Soviet Union by the mid-1970s. Instead of the promised change, Russia was sucked into the deepest economic and social crisis imaginable.

Corrupt government officials did not know what to do anymore and tried to save themselves. It was obvious that society was falling apart, and it was only a matter of time before a major change would come. But nobody knew when or how it would happen. It could come in the form of another revolution and bloody civil war, as had happened in Russia in 1917 and 1918. The Russian people were angry and scared about what their future held. They tried to survive and find solutions for how to exist in such a rotten society. Though all of Russia's people felt this fear and instability, artists were hit especially hard. But it had not always been like this in Russia.

In the beginning of the 20th century, Russia experienced an unprecedented blossoming of all forms of the arts: literature, theater, performing arts, and architecture. St. Petersburg saw the rise of the instrumental school and violin playing especially, a movement led by Leopold Auer, violin virtuoso and phenomenal teacher. This period in Russian culture is often referred to as "The Golden Era." It lasted about 90 years, and the 1970s-80s might be considered its sunset.

The main reason for its dramatic decline was the lack of artistic freedom in a totalitarian society that inevitably manifested in artists searching for a better place for self-expression where they could be appreciated, not persecuted. Jews represented a significant part of the Russian instrumental arts at that time, and the rising anti-Semitism with the threat of physical violence (or worse) left Jews with no choice but to leave their homeland. A new exodus for the Jews was beginning. This movement would dry out a once-fertile soil for the Russian arts.

In the 1970s and 1980s, the great masters of the older generation were still at the wheel of the majestic but already sinking ship of Russian arts. They included pianists Sviatoslav Richter and Emil Gilels, cellists Mstislav Rostropovich and Daniil Shafran, and violinists David Oistrakh and Leonid Kogan.

David Oistrakh was not a child prodigy like most great violinists. His talent took time to develop, and eventually made him one of the most outstanding violinists of the 20th century. His posture always reminded me of a rock. His body was almost stationary during performance; only his hands created amazing virtuoso work, producing each note as big as an apple. Even offstage, his violin was always in his hands, except when he sat down to play chess, and he was an accomplished player. Despite his intensive touring and concert schedule, Oistrakh, being a dedicated teacher, always found time for his students. Even in his 60s, when he was not in good health, he continued to travel relentlessly. When someone once suggested that he should slow down and get some rest, Oistrakh responded, "If I stop playing, I will start thinking. If I start thinking, I will die." One can only speculate what Oistrakh meant by this. Could it have been the fate of his country and his people? The question remains without an answer.

Oistrakh's only son, Igor, became an excellent violinist himself. David Oistrakh mentioned more than once that Igor had much more talent than his father, and if Igor were not so lazy, he would become a better violinist than his father. I heard Igor's wonderful recitals many times in Moscow. He also performed with his father in Mozart's *Sinfonia Concertante,* where David played viola and let Igor play the violin. The ensemble and the quality of both players was remarkable. Many years later I heard Igor and his wife, Natalya

Zertsalova, in a recital in the half-empty Benaroya Hall in Seattle. Igor was unknown to Seattleites but the quality of his playing that night fell short of his father's.

While playing with the orchestra in his later years, Leonid Kogan began the habit of tuning his violin higher than everybody else in the orchestra. His idea was that it would help project the sound of his violin, leaving him to literally play "above" the orchestra. When the orchestra performed some baroque or classical concerto, like one by Vivaldi or Mozart, and the solo violin played in unison with the orchestra, it just sounded out of tune. Nevertheless, Kogan continued to follow his artistic conviction, and nobody dared to tell the great virtuoso that for people with a sense of pitch, listening to him was actually acutely unpleasant.

In 1976, a grand gala concert was organized at the opening of the 25th Congress of the Communist Party of the Soviet Union, the most important political event in the country's life. It was held every five years and attracted guests from almost 100 countries. The best Russian musicians had the "honor" of performing for the top party leaders of the Soviet Union. A gigantic violin ensemble was created to perform Fritz Kreisler's *Preludium and Allegro* in unison. In the first row stood 15 exceptional violinists, mostly winners of international violin competitions, led by Leonid Kogan who played along with the group. Kogan was very energetic, intense, and always appeared angry. Behind that distinguished row stood at least 100 younger students arranged in a semicircle (I was among that group). The ensemble looked and sounded magnificent, but we spent a lot of time practicing how to enter and leave the stage. The music had been learned and memorized long ago, and for the five minutes of Kreisler's piece we spent hours waiting in a crowded room for our turn to go onstage at the Kremlin Palace of Congresses, one of the best Russian architectural achievements, and then many times again going through KGB security. The huge hall with a capacity of 6,000 people was not suited for classical music, but microphones fixed the problem. All of the guests loved our ensemble, and the applause was thunderous.

Six years later, at the age of 58, Leonid Kogan died suddenly while traveling by train to his next concert. His stomach ulcer, from which he had suffered for many years, opened up and there was no doctor around to help him. He lost too much blood and died on the train. Kogan was a great performer of the works of Paganini, who by coincidence also died at age of 58. The great intensity of the artistic life shortened the lives of many wonderful violinists of that time. Boris Gutnikov died at age 55, Mikhail Vaiman at 52, Oleg Kagan at 44, and Julian Sitkovetsky at 33.

Around that time, a few wonderful string quartets were performing regularly in Moscow, among them the distinguished Borodin and Beethoven String Quartets. The latter was also infamous for the bizarre relationship between their first violinist and their cellist. The two men did not talk to each other for 20 years (though they played together in the quartet for more than 30 years). When the first violinist wanted to suggest something during rehearsals, he had to ask the second violinist or the violist to pass the message to the cellist, and the cellist would usually reply back that he would not grant the request.

During my years in Moscow, it was so exciting for me to witness the amazing blooming of the arts, and I had my eye on the violin world in particular. The younger generation of violinists established their position on the concert stages of Moscow and I heard them all: Albert Markov, Nelly Shkolnikova, Boris Gutnikov, Mark Lubotsky, Valery Klimov, Mikhail Vaiman, Mikhail Fichtengolz, and Boris Goldstein. At the Gnessin Musical College while waiting for our next class, we students would listen through the doors to Nelly Shkolnikova and Vladimir Spivakov performing cascades of scales in double stops at turbo speed, showing off and competing with each other. Obviously I favored my highly respected teacher, Nelly Shkolnikova, but it was impossible to distinguish who was who behind closed doors; both violinists were superb virtuosi.

Vladimir Spivakov was an attractive young fellow, just a few years out of the conservatory. He was always surrounded by a cloud of expensive foreign cologne, dressed in imported clothes, and spoke slowly in a very low voice, all of which gave him the aura of an important and mysterious person. Spivakov's class at the Gnessin College consisted mostly of young women, and they were all in love with him.

At one of the recitals Spivakov performed Bach's *Chaconne* for solo violin. Out of youthful bravery, or maybe still searching for the right bowings, he played all the chords upside down, starting the piece on an up-bow. To everybody in the hall, this looked like an almost criminal offense to the tradition of *Chaconne* performance. I figured he was just showing off and wanted to demonstrate that he could play everything upside down and still perform perfectly from a technical standpoint, and indeed he played with precision. But his performance planted a seed of doubt in my heart about Spivakov's talent. I felt that a person with a natural sense of musicianship would not need to present such an experiment in front of an audience. Later I learned that my feelings about Spivakov were justified; over time, his performances lost the charm they once had, and he never truly grew into a major violin star. I was pleased that my intuition was correct, but was more disappointed that such a fine violinist whom everybody loved did not meet our expectations.

Another star of the Russian violin world was Victor Tretyakov, who was not yet 20 when he won the first prize at the third International Tchaikovsky Competition in 1966. His brilliant live recording of the Paganini First Violin Concerto from the final round of the competition still remains one of the best recordings of this virtuoso piece. Tretyakov unmistakably had the potential to grow into a remarkable artist, but unfortunately his propensity for drinking prevented him from building a more successful career. Tretyakov's father was a well-known figure in Moscow. He was the only one who built fancy and durable handmade violin cases, but you had to wait many months in line to get one. (He worked by himself in his tiny kitchen and when I visited his apartment, the first thing I noticed when he opened the door was the strong smell of glue, which forced me to take a step back for a moment before reentering the apartment.) At that time in Russia it was only possible to buy low-quality and primitive-looking violin cases; the first imported violin cases of much better quality were just starting to come in from the German Democratic Republic (East Germany), but for a high price. Forty years later I still have two of Tretyakov's cases, both in excellent condition: one single and another double for two violins with beautiful scarlet plush on the inside.

In the 1970s and 1980s, the youngest generation of violinists was slowly taking over the stage. I never missed the student recitals of

David Oistrakh and Yuri Yankelevich, two titans of Russian violin pedagogy. This is where I first heard the talents of brilliant virtuoso Philippe Hirschhorn, who would later go on to win the prestigious International Queen Elizabeth Music Competition (he would die prematurely at age of 50 of a brain tumor), and Oleg Kagan (a musician with a very sophisticated style who soon would become a partner in chamber music with Sviatoslav Richter), Boris Belkin, Victoria Mullova, Liana Isakadze, and many others.

The violinists who were accepted into the Moscow conservatory and were lucky enough to become students of Yuri Yankelevich took lessons once a week with his primary assistant, Maya Glezarova. She was a most ferocious teacher, a notorious character of the Moscow conservatory. Before the lesson students would stand at the door of her classroom trembling with fear. She was extremely demanding, and one would require a miracle in order to meet her astronomically high standards. It was not unusual for the door to her classroom to suddenly swing wide open, her hands throwing fistfuls of sheet music into the hallway. Her yelling could be heard in the lobby, "Get out of here! Get back to practicing, and don't come back until you've learned those passages!" Her diatribes sent the poor terrorized students, pale and shaking, running out of the room and scrambling to pick their music up off the ground. It came as no surprise that the next time the students returned to their lessons, they performed the passages perfectly.

All these wonderful young players were constantly preparing themselves for international competitions, going through the hard labor of hundreds and hundreds of hours of intense practicing, like athletes training for the Olympics. The competitions were extremely difficult, but they could open doors to a successful lifelong career. The highest professional level was as important as the physical endurance of the performer.

One of David Oistrakh's talented students, Victor Pikaizen, was busy preparing for the Paganini Competition in Genoa, Italy. Since Genoa has a much warmer climate than Moscow and high humidity (the competition was held in September), Pikaizen decided to practice all the extremely difficult Paganini concertos and caprices dressed in a winter coat buttoned to the top, and lying on his back in bed. It was truly an awkward practicing position. He was sweating like a boxer in the ring. Who gave him this advice? Who knows, but it worked! After passing all three rounds, Pikaizen won the first prize at the competition. On his return home he frequently played all 24 Paganini *Caprices* in one concert program, also becoming the first Russian violinist who recorded all the Paganini *Caprices*. The recording is of impressive quality, and became a milestone in Russian discography.

18 · Conductors and Their Orchestras

In my more than two decades (1969-1990) of living in Moscow, the epicenter of Russian cultural life, I developed a special interest in conducting and started to follow the concerts of the famous conductors of the time. Russia had a wonderful school of conducting. In the 1970s and 1980s the Moscow and Leningrad (as it was named at the time) chamber and symphony orchestras were led by a group of extraordinary conductors.

In 1955, Rudolf Barshai founded and for many years was the only conductor of the Moscow Chamber Orchestra, making the group one of the finest and on par with the best European chamber orchestras. Barshai was an excellent violist himself. He made a few wonderful recordings, and his rendition of Bach's *Chaconne* transcribed for viola is outstanding. The Moscow Chamber Orchestra practiced every day for many hours. There were full orchestra rehearsals, then there were sectionals, then musicians practiced their parts in smaller groups like string quartets, and sometimes they even practiced one on one with the section leader. Their precision of intonation, unity of bowings, and ensemble sound set the highest standards for orchestral playing. Their concerts were always sold out, and I managed to attend many of them. They made many outstanding recordings, among them *The Four Seasons* by Antonio Vivaldi, with brilliant solos by concertmaster Yevgeny Smirnov. I consider this performance a virtuosic masterpiece. Later, Barshai decided that he no longer wanted to deal with the Russian political and musical bureaucracy, and in 1977 he left Russia. He wrote his autobiography, *The Note*, which was adapted into a movie of the same title in the year of his death, 2010.

Valery Gergiev was just starting his career during my Moscow years, and I played a concert with him once in a casual orchestra. That concert did not leave a strong impression on my memory since we only played some pieces of young modern Russian composers. Gergiev rose to the top of the conducting world years later, and now leads the Mariinsky Theater in St. Petersburg and guest conducts with the best orchestras. His super-busy schedule has become legendary, and he was recently recognized as the highest-paid conductor of all time. He is definitely a unique figure in the musical world, and has grown into a remarkable musician with an instantly recognizable style. I met Valery Gergiev again in 1990 at a private party in San Francisco in the home of my future friend, Leon Igudesman. Gergiev was guest conducting the San Francisco Opera.

Yevgeny Svetlanov was, for many years, the music director of the State Academic Symphony Orchestra of the USSR, formally the main Russian symphony orchestra. He was a very serious musician and especially good with interpretations of Russian music, over which he was considered to have indisputable authority. Svetlanov was very strict and had a tyrannical personality. It was a time when the conductor had absolute power over the orchestra and his musicians (and actually, things haven't changed much in Russia since). The following incident illustrates the totalitarian nature and dictatorial approach of the conductor's profession.

Mark Gorenstein played in the first violin section of the State Academic Symphony Orchestra. He was a good violinist, and also did some conducting on the side. One day he approached Svetlanov and told him that one of the instruments did not sound right in one of the movements. He suggested it was probably a misprint in the part, but something sounded wrong. This kind of comment could imply that Svetlanov himself had not heard it, missing the potential error in the score. Gorenstein hardly finished his report when Svetlanov called up the orchestra manager, and, pointing to Gorenstein, exclaimed, "Get him out of here!" Gorenstein was fired on the spot. A few years later, after Svetlanov died, Gorenstein was appointed the chief conductor of that same orchestra. Now that's irony! The real end of the story is that nine years after Gorenstein's appointment, the musicians signed a petition to the Minister of Culture asking him to fire Gorenstein. The grounds for that request were based on the unbearable working conditions (Gorenstein constantly humiliated, threatened, and fired a lot of orchestra musicians during his tenure), as well as the declining quality of the formerly renowned orchestra. The Minister of Culture had no choice but to dismiss Gorenstein. Most likely the rule "violence creates more violence" was true in this case – or was it simply karma?

Yevgeny Mravinsky serves as another example of the despotic conductor, though the remarkable results he achieved often outweighed the cost of those achievements. Mravinsky led the Leningrad Philharmonic Orchestra for 50 years, holding his musicians in strict control while simultaneously generating a deep respect from his colleagues. He made his orchestra a world-class ensemble, probably the best in Russia at the time.

Vladimir Spivakov founded the "Moscow Virtuosi" in 1979. This group was intended to be more entertaining in repertoire than the Moscow Chamber Orchestra, with its more academic approach. Spivakov's popularity at the time was so high that he was able to convince the best musicians from Moscow orchestras to leave their steady jobs to start the new group, which promised to be more exciting and even better paid. Spivakov succeeded in the latter but the repertoire of the group became quite narrow, not to mention that it carried a certain banality in its artistic interpretations. Eventually there was a big change in personnel as a result of sour relations between the musicians and Spivakov, but at its very beginning this smaller version of the symphony orchestra became very popular, and moved its way up in cultural life, both nationally and internationally.

As a gesture of personal and artistic competition with Spivakov, the young, brilliant violist Yuri Bashmet founded his own group, "Moscow Soloists." It was smaller in size than the Moscow Virtuosi and focused more on chamber repertoire. Bashmet often played solos with his group, but in later years the quality of his performances declined. On top of that, his relationship with the orchestra soured, and as some of musicians stated, this was due to the personal qualities of their leader.

Kirill Kondrashin (1914-1981) led the orchestra of the Moscow Philharmonic for 15 years. He was a very good conductor and musician, highly respected by his colleagues. His interpretations of European masters were profound and intelligent. At the first International Tchaikovsky Competition in Moscow in 1958 he performed with Van Cliburn, which brought Cliburn the First Prize and Gold Medal and also gave Kondrashin a great reputation, leading to recordings and tours with Cliburn in America. In 1978 Kondrashin defected while touring in Europe. His exile to Eastern

Europe was short; he died three years later at the age of 67. The Moscow Philharmonic Orchestra's Associate Concertmaster, the very fine violinist Emanuel Borok, immigrated to Israel. He played for a few years as the Associate Concertmaster with the Boston Symphony, and later won a concertmaster position with the Dallas Symphony. Borok was a friend of Kostya's, with whom I played for 10 years in the Moscow State Symphony. He helped me with valuable professional advice when I first arrived in the United States.

At the age of 29, Yuri Simonov was appointed chief conductor of the Bolshoi Theatre, becoming the youngest chief conductor in the history of the Bolshoi. His conducting technique was superb from a professional point of view, but he overdid his gestures to the point of caricature. His rehearsals were long and intense and the shows were no fun to play. He became a tyrant to the musicians of the orchestra. They disliked him and lived in fear for years until Simonov was replaced by another conductor.

Gennady Rozhdestvensky had held the position of chief conductor of the Symphony Orchestra of the All-Union Radio and Television in Moscow since 1961. It was a well-paid group. Rozhdestvensky had a wonderful relationship with his musicians; he was a good man with a positive personality. He had the rare ability to establish contact with people, whether they were musicians or the audience. The autocratic system and music director's power did not corrupt him. Musicians also loved him because he did not like to rehearse too much, unlike many other conductors who would use their rehearsal time up to the very last second. Rozhdestvensky would come to the first rehearsal with his orchestra, read through a Tchaikovsky symphony or other standard piece on the program, and would say, "I know this music. You know this music. I will see you at the concert." And the concerts were so inspiring! Musicians obviously tried their very best and the orchestra sounded wonderful. This approach worked very well with the orchestras Rozhdestvensky knew, but his phenomenal qualities did not always serve him well. Once he had to conduct an orchestra in Stockholm, and used the same rehearsal "technique" (since the piece they had to play was well known both to him and to the orchestra). After the first rehearsal he cancelled all remaining rehearsals, feeling that they were not necessary, but the orchestra union protested his decision and asked him to conduct all rehearsals as stated in his contract. Rozhdestvensky refused, arguing that it was not necessary for the orchestra to practice more then he thought was needed, and that this would only make the orchestra tired and bored and this, inevitably, would result in a less exciting performance. Two different points of view clashed, and no solution was found. Rozhdestvensky refused to complete his rehearsals, which brought his engagement with the orchestra to an end, resulting in the cancellation of the concerts as well as his contract.

Rozhdestvensky was a very popular conductor in the West and was often invited to conduct orchestras abroad. One time after guest conducting with a European orchestra, he returned to Moscow to discover that he had to face an enormous personal challenge. It was 1974. The dark cloud of anti-Semitism hung over Russia. Rozhdestvensky was called to a meeting with a KGB official who was overlooking the All-Union Radio and Television (one of the important tools in Soviet propaganda). Rozhdestvensky was told that he had to get rid of the Jewish musicians in his orchestra. At that time 42 people, almost half of the orchestra, were Jews. Rozhdestvensky refused to heed this order. Under continuous pressure, he had no choice but to resign from his position; he would never go against his conscience. Another conductor, Vladimir Fedoseyev, was appointed in Rozhdestvensky's place. Fedoseyev had absolutely no experience as a symphony orchestra conductor. He had been directing an orchestra of Russian folk instruments, but had a close relationship with the Minister of Culture. Fedoseyev immediately "cleaned up" his new orchestra, firing all the Jews, but following the order to leave one single Jewish musician: the principal cellist. This exception was made just to show that there was no anti-Semitism in the organization. All of Moscow's musical intelligentsia were furious at such a monstrous act, and some of the orchestra's musicians even resigned in protest. They did not want to work with Fedoseyev. Obviously nothing changed, and the decision was final.

After losing his job with the Radio and Television Orchestra, Rozhdestvensky was invited to take over the orchestra at the Chamber Opera Theater, where operas of smaller caliber were staged with a small orchestra, small cast, and minimal set design. It was a more modernistic theater where one could hear operas that would never make their way to the more traditional stage of the Bolshoi Theater.

On a few occasions I had the honor to play under the direction of Gennady Rozhdestvensky. I clearly remember the time we performed *The Nose* by Dmitri Shostakovich at the Chamber Opera Theater. The music was tricky, but trickier yet was the fact that the orchestra was extremely small – only 15 people (the score required 40 musicians). We sat in a tiny orchestra pit and every musician could hear each note from each of his or her colleagues. Every part was so exposed. I was playing on the first stand of first violins (there were only three first violins), literally under the nose of Rozhdestvensky. He was not a tall man and his round glasses made his resemblance to the composer Sergei Prokofiev even stronger. Rozhdestvensky had a long baton, longer than most other conductors had. He conducted using mostly his wrists and every move of his baton was absolutely clear. It danced in the air like an acrobat at the circus, pointing precisely to the right instrument at the right time, giving each musician the cue for their entrance. Rozhdestvensky always conducted with a smile on his face and looked directly into the eyes of the players, which musicians liked a lot. Rozhdestvensky had a phenomenal memory and great conducting skills, but one thing he could not stand was to see a musician counting the bars of a rest. This offended Rozhdestvensky, and if he saw such a thing he would say, "Don't count! I will show you your entrance." And he never failed to do so. This kind of help from the conductor was very valuable and appreciated, especially in such complex music as the Shostakovich. Rozhdestvensky's gift for sight-reading was legendary. He could open any new score, look at it for a few moments, and start conducting with total confidence, noting even the smallest details.

One thing about Rozhdestvensky remains a mystery to me: in later years when he conducted standard symphonic compositions like Tchaikovsky or Beethoven symphonies, he literally had his nose buried in the score for the duration of the performance. He would rarely lift his head to look at the musicians, though he always managed to give the correct cues with his long baton. After over 50 years of conducting those pieces, he had probably memorized them; it would be expected from an experienced conductor, especially one of such caliber. Nevertheless, his head was helplessly hidden in the score.

Gennady Rozhdestvensky made a huge contribution to Russian musical life. He introduced a large pool of Russian and European lesser-known modern compositions to Moscow audiences, often accompanying his performances with fascinating lectures. The man had an encyclopedic knowledge; he did in Moscow what Leonard Bernstein did in New York: educating thousands and thousands of people, broadening their knowledge, and shaping their perspective about the music. Rozhdestvensky's unique book, *Triangles*, reflects his wide spectrum of interests in painting, literature, and music, and shows the deep connection between all forms of art.

19 · My New Place

After my divorce in 1983 I found myself as a single man renting my own place for the first time. It was a small room in a communal flat that I shared with an old woman and her alcoholic son. The room was the same size as the one I had rented while studying at the Gnessin School, but this time it was my own! I immediately redecorated it. I learned how to put up new wallpaper by myself, bought new, modern furniture and new drapes, and put a comfy Persian-style rug on the floor next to my bed. Besides the neighbors who were anti-Semitic, the other disadvantage was that the room was halfway below ground level. Out the window I could only see shoes and boots scuffling back and forth. In the end I did not really mind it; I even created a special game around trying to guess the identity of the owner of the red high heels or the brand new sneakers, and what kind of life was behind them. This pastime made me think of the Japanese writer Kobo Abe, whose novels were very popular in Russia in the 70s. I remember his brilliant novel, *The Box Man*, in which a man lives in a box and watches the outside world through a hole. My new girlfriends liked my place very much, and they also enjoyed my cooking. Along with other dishes, I learned how to make a delicious barley soup. At that time it was my signature dish. (No, no. I am not giving away my recipe that easily!)

20 · Larisa

I could not take my eyes off of her. She had come to play with the Moscow State Symphony as a substitute violinist for a program, and at the first intermission I rushed over to my manager to ask who she was. There was no way she hadn't seen me staring at her every time she passed me by. The way she walked was intoxicating; she moved as if she carried a mystery within her, and she was very aware of this. Her gorgeous olive eyes and pitch-black hair attracted me powerfully. I fell in love. I was not a bad-looking fellow myself, as others had attested, so I thought I stood a chance. With my heart beating like a drum I approached her and opened my mouth to speak. I couldn't recognize the sound of my own voice. I sounded like I had just recovered from a severe cold. But it seemed that she understood my intentions, and allowed me to walk her back to her apartment, though I did not come in. Our romance was a classic one, and soon I knew that Larisa had also fallen in love with me.

Larisa

Meeting Larisa opened up a whole new world to me: a world of people who wanted to leave the Soviet Union, but were not allowed to do so. Larisa and her parents had applied for emigration in 1978. At that time, the USSR was enmeshed in a political game with the United States and peoples' human rights were at stake. Under pressure from the West, the Soviet government let some people leave the country, but as soon as the political climate changed, the emigration gates would shut. Thousands of Russian Jews watched their dreams of living in the free world collapse like a house of cards. The doors were closed for the unforeseen future, perhaps even forever.

People, however, did not know this, and continued to stand in long lines at the OVIR (*Otdel Viz i Registratsii* /Office of Visas and Registration), the organization responsible for processing emigration requests. The answer to all requests was a firm "NO" accompanied by ridiculous reasons. Larisa's family's request was denied for "security" reasons. The letter they received stated that her parents worked in an industry that required 10 years of security clearance. Their world fell apart; they lost their jobs with no hope for future employment. They became "enemies of society," and were granted the title *refuznik*. That is what people were called who applied to leave but were not allowed. These people did not realize that they involuntary contributed to the Russian language the word that became the most popular at that time – "*otkaznik*" or "refuznik."

Since Russians could easily distinguish people of Slavic origin from Jews by their facial features, it was common to hear on the street or on public transportation, "You, *zhid*, go back to your Israel!" Any response to the insult would be an excellent excuse to get punched in the face. Anti-Semitism was rampant. The economic situation in the whole country had become unbearable. There were no basic medications, the food supply was worse than ever, and people were growing angrier. A scapegoat needed to be identified and the Jews had conveniently filled this role for centuries. The Russian government was spreading a rumor that it was the Jews who had destroyed the economy. A snowball of hatred against the Jews grew bigger and bigger with each passing day. More rumors started up about the threat of possible *pogroms* (an organized massacre of an ethnic group, in particular that of Jews in Russia or Eastern Europe). *Pogroms* had long been a part of the classical Russian political tradition.

Inflation was growing faster than bamboo and people soon

learned that they could buy things on the black market at enormous prices. Do you need shoes for winter? Sorry, nothing in the store. But it's not a problem, because we can get you any shoes you like. It will cost you a month's salary though. Fresh fruits or vegetables? Not until summer and only through the back door. This was a time when the famous Russian saying, "You don't need to have 100 rubles, but you do need to have 100 friends" became truly applicable. At least a few of your 100 friends would have connections to the supply world.

Larisa's family had miserable savings that melted away quickly. Her parents still couldn't find jobs and continued to send their papers to the OVIR, only to receive the same rejection letter over and over again. Time was crawling by very slowly and everyone was mired in uncertainty. But even in that scary situation there were some brave individuals who were not afraid to help the Jews. After applying to more than a dozen public schools, Larisa got lucky and finally found a job teaching music in an elementary school.

I had never before thought about leaving my country. I had a good job, a good position in the orchestra, and many friends. My orchestra was touring abroad, so we could bring imported goods back to Russia, sell them, and double our salary. Since there was a shortage in Russia of literally everything, we could bring anything back for resale. The best profit one could make was on American jeans and CD players, as well as anything for the ladies, from cosmetics to underwear. Russian women wanted to look "in style" and they were our best buyers. I made enough money to buy a condo in a new 12-story building, and that's precisely when the beautiful Larisa came into my life and changed it forever. I learned that even though my life was good according to existing standards, it might not be like that the next day. There were no guarantees when it came to our basic human rights. It took some time for Larisa to open my eyes and convince me to join her in her efforts to leave the country.

Meanwhile, we got married and Larisa became pregnant. She developed a condition that threatened to cause premature labor, but there were no medications available at the pharmacies. We continued to send papers to the OVIR, and one day in November 1989 a miracle happened: we were finally granted permission to leave the country! A few days later we received an invitation from the American Embassy to enter the country as members of a *refuznik* group consisting of a few dozen families who had also been awaiting permission to leave the Soviet Union since the end of the 1970s. It was now 1990, a very strange time. The new Soviet leader, Mikhail Gorbachev, suggested a brilliant and dangerous idea, one that would have seemed impossible given the Great October Socialist Revolution of 1917. He decided to break up the Soviet Empire. One of his first steps was to give people certain freedoms, and to let them live in the country of their choice. This idea soon became a reality, and would earn Gorbachev a Nobel Peace Prize.

21 · Silent Revolution

Just six months earlier, another important event had occurred. It did not have the magnitude of the collapse of the USSR, but it did have a very deep impact on Moscow's artistic life.

Our orchestra could no longer tolerate its Music Director, Veronica Dudarova. Twenty-nine years of oppression had taken its toll on people. Her complete lack of professionalism mixed with her thirst for power and dictatorship drove people crazy. The musicians' mood and morale were below any acceptable standards. The situation had come to a boiling point; we knew that things could not continue on in this way.

Dudarova had very strong connections in the Ministry of Culture, which controlled all artistic life in the USSR. With one word she could easily fire the entire orchestra. Something like that had already happened in the past when a group of musicians wrote a letter to the Ministry of Culture, stating all of the "artistic crimes" of Dudarova. To their surprise, when they came to work the next day, they discovered that they had all been fired. Someone had reported them.

This time all the musicians were totally united. All of us wanted Dudarova out. On that memorable day, we all came to work as usual, took our instruments out of their cases, the first oboist played an "A" and the concertmaster tuned the orchestra. Dudarova came out of her room, got on the podium, did not greet the orchestra (we could tell she was angry), sat in her chair, raised her hands, and gave an upbeat. We were trembling in unison, but nobody lifted their instrument. The orchestra refused to play with its conductor. Nothing like this had ever happened in the history of Soviet musical life. A silent revolution! She was not expecting silence from the orchestra, but refused to believe that she was in the midst of a coup. Dropping her hands, she looked at the orchestra like a snake at a mouse, hypnotizing us with fear for a few intense seconds that felt like an eternity. Slowly she descended from the podium, went to her room, collected her belongings, and left forever.

We were all scared to death. What would happen next? The whole situation felt unreal. The next day the orchestra wrote a letter to the Minister of Culture stating what had happened, and all 90 orchestra members signed it. We asked that Pavel Kogan, a young, talented violinist and conductor (as well as the son of world famous violinist Leonid Kogan) be appointed our new Music Director. The Minister signed the letter.

22 · *Emigration*

After we received permission from the OVIR to leave the country, the first thing our homeland did was take away our passports and revoke our citizenship. At that point, we did not have any identification. In case we were stopped for any reason by the militzia, we would be in trouble. We became citizens of the Universe! Before we were granted entry to the US, which came to us as a total surprise, we received visas to Israel.

Israel was the only country to which Russian Jews were allowed to emigrate. Jews had to provide a reason they wanted to leave the USSR to the government, and the Soviet bureaucrats created the reason that would satisfy the authorities: reconnection with the family. The assumption that every Jew had a relative living in Israel was a farce. Like most emigrants, we did not have any relatives in that faraway country. Nevertheless, one day we received an invitation from our "relatives" from Israel for a reunion. As I said, we had never even heard their names, but that *vizov* (request to come) at that time was enough for the OVIR to let us go. We passed the required medical tests, filled out tons of other papers, and started... shopping. Yes, shopping!

To begin with, we could not take our violins with us: everything that was appraised above 1,000 rubles was considered a Russian treasure and was not allowed to be taken out of the country with emigrants. I had an Italian violin and Larisa had a good French one, which were definitely worth more than 1,000 rubles each. We had to quickly sell both violins, but for a purchase price in rubles, which were worth pennies on the dollar.[5]

We bought two freshly made Russian violins that sounded as if somebody had poured water into them, and they were appraised within the allowed sum. Then we realized that we were only al-

---

5 At that time there was a currency exchange technique in Russia. Before leaving the country we had to sell practically everything we had. But because rubles had no value outside of Russia, people bought black market dollars in exchange for rubles, yet they still could not declare that at customs and take those dollars with them at the border since it was illegal. So we were selling our rubles in Russia and then somebody would give us dollars when we arrived in the US. We simply had to trust these mysterious people who were the masterminds of this exchange process. Somehow it worked, and when we arrived in the US we were given a few hundred dollars from people totally unknown to us.

lowed to take one violin per family. Don't ask why; Russian emigration rules: one violin per family. We got the second violin back two years later from my sister and my parents, who left the country six months after us. They went to Israel, taking the second violin with them. Until then Larisa would borrow my violin, since I was practicing all the time.

Shopping was kind of fun. We were told what we should take to Israel to resell there in order to make some extra money. The most ridiculous sounding advice was to buy ballet shoes, and as many as possible. It seemed that all of Israel was taking ballet lessons. Then don't forget the heater for your own use: most floors in Israel were made of stone to keep people cool in the summer heat, but in winter the floors were terribly cold. Our Moscow apartment began to look like a warehouse. The next ridiculous thing was that after we got permission from the US government to come to America, we had to sell all this stuff. Quite a few people visited us in those days, people who were going to Israel, not to America, and our apartment quickly became empty.

During this time, Larisa spent a lot of time in the hospital. Her medical condition meant that when she was at home she had to lie with her legs up to prevent premature labor. Now that we had our visas to enter the United States, we faced a new problem: we could not find transportation. Without proper documentation and identification, it was impossible to buy plane tickets to New York. A former colleague's wife who worked for Aeroflot managed to work her way around the rules and bought us tickets. We were so grateful. The day had come.

It was February 21, 1990. In a few months the USSR would collapse, but nobody knew about that yet, except possibly for Gorbachev. We arrived at the airport with plenty of time to spare, and the customs officials tried to humiliate us as much as they could, rifling through all our belongings as if we had something to hide. They were upset when they failed to find any prohibited items. Finally, we were at the passport control booth. "Passports!" the young sergeant yelled. Of course we did not have passports. Instead I had a large sealed brown envelope with the paperwork from the American Embassy inside that was only to be opened inside the US. The sergeant looked at the envelope and asked, "What is this?" I tried to explain. He said that we could not cross the border without passports, and he was right. As I was told later, we were the first family going directly to the US. It was a new route for emigration, and people at border control had not seen this type of documentation before. The only proof that this envelope belonged to us was four black and white photographs, all differently sized and glued to the upper right corner of the envelope like four stamps.

Time stopped. I was afraid that Larisa would go into labor right there. For a few minutes nothing happened. The sergeant was totally confused. Finally, he asked his supervisor, the captain, to come and decide what to do. The captain walked in with his perfect KGB officer posture. I told him our story, and he examined the envelope from both sides. He stared at us for a few long seconds.

"---[6] with them! Let them go!" That was the sweetest swear word I had ever heard in my life. We crossed the fat red line, never to look back.

End of Part One

---

6 Unprintable Russian curse word

Photo Album: Russia

Age 3

Looks like I forgot my lines!

Violin Ensemble at Frunze Music School (I am fourth from the right)

At Frunze Music School in the company of two fairies

*Caricature of me (age 17) by my
friend Nicolai Gorbunov*

*My father with his military deco-
rations from World War II*

МИНИСТЕРСТВО КУЛЬТУРЫ РСФСР
ГЛАВНОЕ УПРАВЛЕНИЕ УЧЕБНЫХ ЗАВЕДЕНИЙ И КАДРОВ

Московская _____ средняя специальная музыкальная

школа *им. Гнесина* при _____

УДОСТОВЕРЕНИЕ

к аттестату № *083420*

Настоящее удостоверение выдано *Миропольскому Михаилу*

Петровичу, родившемуся в 19*55* году, в том, что он____

в 19*69* поступил____ и в 19*72* году окончил____ полный курс

названной школы по специальности *скрипка*_____

и обнаружил____следующие знания по предметам:

Специальность	*5 (отлично)*
Камерный ансамбль	*5 (отлично)*
Оркестр	*5 (отлично)*
Аккомпанемент	—
Общее фортепиано	*5 (отлично)*
Сольфеджио	*5 (отлично)*
Гармония	*5 (отлично)*
Анализ музыкальных произведений	—
Музыкальная литература	*5 (отлично)*

Директор школы ____
Руководитель отдела ____

24. июня 1972 г.

Московская типография Гознака. 1961 г.

Report card from my final year at Gnessin Musical School

My portrait by Russian painter Chemodurov

Unknown artist sketches my portrait

On tour with Moscow State Symphony in Venezuela

Concert program of the String Quartet of the
Union of Composers of the USSR

Program insert for the concert of the String Quartet of the
Union of Composers of the USSR in Moscow Conservatory

*On the tour with Moscow State Symphony in Prague
(I am behind Russian composer Tikhon Khrennikov
and conductor Dudarova)*

With my father and mother

With my sister

PART TWO: AMERICA

Prelude: Musical Diaspora

What happened in Russia in the 20th century was an unprecedented event in the history of mankind and a huge tragedy for the Russian people and their culture. The Bolshevik Revolution in 1917 triggered a Russian cultural exodus. From 1920 to 1930, top scientists and the best artists started fleeing the country due to its unpredictable future. Others who believed in the new socialist form of society stayed, but lost their artistic freedom, and eventually paid a high price for their trust. The luckiest remained alive and were allowed to continue their work in the metal cage of communist regulations. The less fortunate ended up in Gulags.

World War II and the following two decades of my country's recovery and reconstruction sent dissident thinking underground. The next wave of mass emigration continued through the 70s, and then after 13 years of a "locked" society, emigration began again in the 90s. It is extremely hard to evaluate and impossible to overestimate the degree of loss sustained by Russian culture in the last century. Naming some of the extraordinary artists who left the country would be unfair to the others; naming all would create an endless list. I was witness to the last two waves of emigration, and became a part of the last one myself.

Both of my violin teachers, Professor Piotr Bondarenko and Nelli Shkolnikova, as well as many of my colleagues from the Moscow State Symphony Orchestra, left Russia. They settled mostly in Israel, Spain, Germany, France, and the United States. I believe that every major European or American orchestra has a Russian musician or even a few (like the Seattle Symphony). Bondarenko found a new homeland in Israel. Shkolnikova, after more than decade of being barred from leaving the USSR, defected to former West Germany and later taught in the United States at the prestigious Indiana University. In my long telephone conversations with her, she complained that her students did not have a lot of talent. She was obviously missing the old days when she taught at the Gnessin Institute of Music in Moscow.

The story of twenty leading musicians including the concertmaster of the Leningrad Philharmonic who one day notified the administration of their decision to resign from the orchestra and leave the country shook the musical community. Such was an un-heard-of event in the history of musical emigration, and it caused irreparable damage to that fine orchestra.

The assimilation of Russian musicians into American orchestras was (and continues to be) a difficult process. For some Russians, the psychological adaptation to the new culture of the American orchestra became an insurmountable obstacle. Especially when it comes to string players, at the root of the American orchestra lies a polished and perfect ensemble, a very different approach from our training in Russia. The Russian school of violin and string playing in general focused primarily on the rich tone of the instrument, bright personality, and profound musicianship, which are exactly the qualities that are not high on the priority list of the American orchestra.

Twentieth century Russia was blessed with an army of brilliant and talented people. Almost a century later, its famous ballet still impresses audiences all over the world, but the country is well past the glorious time when it produced some of the best instrumental players. There are no more new Heifetzes, Elmans or Zimbalists coming from Russia.

23 · San Francisco

The flight was long and exhausting, and I spent the entire time worrying about Larisa, but she made it to New York. Representatives from a Jewish organization met us at the airport, and I gave them the brown envelope. While we were waiting for the paperwork, a middle-aged woman approached us and asked if we had relatives in New York. We said that we were going to San Francisco to meet our sponsor.

"How pregnant is your wife?" she asked. "Seven and a half months," I said.

"At this stage of pregnancy, they will not allow you to board the plane. That's the rule," the woman said.

"But we don't know anybody in New York, and our sponsor is already waiting for us in San Francisco! What are we going to do?" After everything we had been through, we were not expecting this.

"You have only one way. Tell them that your wife is five months pregnant." I told myself, "I don't have a choice. This will be my first and last lie in this land." I did as she suggested but was ashamed to have done so.

My first impressions of America were acoustic in nature.

Upon our arrival, Genrich, our sponsor, met us at the San Francisco airport. We put our modest luggage in the spacious trunk of his Ford Taurus, and headed to the place where we would be staying. I sat in the back with my in-laws; Larisa and her nearly eight-month belly took the front seat. We got on the freeway and the conversation began. Even though we were excited, the 23-hour flight across the Atlantic had worn us out. As we spoke in Russian I noticed a strange accent in Genrich's voice. There was something unusual in the way he stretched his vowels. It gave the words a sing-song quality that we did not have in Russia. In a few years I would also pick up this same accent, and later yet I would hear the same singing Russian when my son spoke to me. Strangely neither Larisa nor Evelina seemed to adopt the accent.

Genrich's calm voice gradually receded into the background,

and another sound caught my attention. From time to time I would hear a strange rumble coming from underneath the car. The sound reminded me of a snare drum or a timpani roll, and every time it happened the car would vibrate in unison with the sound.

For as long as I can remember I have been very sensitive to sound, and it occupies a special part of my memory. I feel that hearing is perhaps even more important to me than it is to other people. I am quite certain that this quality, this sharpened awareness and greater audible comprehension, has helped me become a musician. I experience the world around me through sound, and when I came to America the sounds I heard were very new to me.

The mystery of the automobile's rumble would soon be resolved when I began taking driving lessons. It was the raised pavement markers that created the rolling sound and made the car vibrate. In Russia there were no such bumps on the roads, just worn-out painted lines.

Since that evening this sound was imprinted in my memory as my first impression in America. I can hear it still as I write these lines. I can remember that evening drive, the vibrations, and the butterflies in my stomach. It was all part of this feeling of the unknown, a new enchanted world that lay ahead of us – a new life in a new country. I had left behind 35 years of my life, and was about to begin again from scratch. A new day with an ocean of new impressions was waiting. Tomorrow I would feel like a baby trying to stand up and take his first steps. From this shift in perspective, the world would suddenly look very different, and feeling unstable on my feet, I would fall down. Making my way back up again, I would begin anew.

For the first few weeks, we stayed with our relative (the sponsor's mom), while Genrich looked for an apartment for us to rent. It was an interesting time of adaptation. In the morning when I looked out the window, I felt that this could not be real; it must be just a dream where I was a passive observer. The street names and the houses looked weird; I could not recognize the smells and sounds. On the street people were always courteously giving me room to pass by, looking in my eyes and saying, "Hi!" or "How are you?" I took these greetings seriously and tried to answer every time, but before I even opened my mouth, they were gone. My "good morning" or "good afternoon" with my perfect British accent did not make much of an impression.

Before coming to America I thought that my English was very good, and indeed it was, but for some reason I could not really understand what people were saying to me. I also got the feeling that they didn't understand me very well. They were just very nice and tried to help. I realized that I could not communicate with people on the level I had expected. It was a different English than the one I had learned at school, and the linguistic difficulties were a big unexpected stress added to my immigration cart.

The American government granted us refugee status, which guaranteed us state support and health insurance for a certain time, a green card in a year, and citizenship in five years.

24 · Evelina

On March 15, 1990 at around 7:00 in the evening, my daughter decided to become the first American citizen in our family. When Larisa's water broke, I called 911, and within just a few minutes our apartment suddenly felt very small. Three huge firemen with their gear and two men in white coats entered the room, and helped Larisa get to the ambulance. I was holding Larisa's hand all the way, and when we arrived at the hospital they told me to put on special shoes and a white robe.

"What for?" I asked.

"Aren't you going to be present at the labor?" I felt that somebody had hit me in the stomach. Back in Russia nobody except the doctor was allowed to be present during labor, and I did not know that I would actually be expected to do a husband's duty here at this time.

The magic happened very quickly. My baby girl gave a healthy high-pitched scream, got cleaned up, weighed, and returned to her mother's arms. It was a miracle, and I was still reeling from the fact that it happened in my presence. We quickly agreed on the baby's name. Evelina (or Eva) had dark hair, and since she was premature (her weight was just above 2 kg – 4 pounds), she stayed in the hospital for a few more days, during which time some kind people and a Jewish organization helped us get a crib and some other things for our newborn.

Upon the baby's return to our apartment, it suddenly became noisier than before. Even though Eva did not cry much, she still did her part, as any baby would do. Amazingly, Eva reacted to my practicing. Whenever she showed discomfort and was becoming cranky, I would get my violin and start playing anything (most often excerpts for auditions). She looked at me with her big eyes trying to get me into focus, and immediately stopped crying. I already had an audience! But not everybody in our apartment building had the same level of approval regarding my practicing. Even though I tried not to practice loudly, and was always finished practicing by 9:30 p.m., the neighbors were often angrily hitting the connecting walls or just knocking at our front door to complain.

One day the fire alarm in the building went off. I dropped the violin, grabbed Eva, and ran outside with Larisa and her parents onto the street. There had been a minor fire, fortunately not in our apartment. All the tenants were waiting outside while the firemen were doing their

My daughter Evelina, who will soon pick up the violin

job. It was getting late, and the baby and her parents were growing hungry, but no one was allowed back inside until the smoke had cleared. After we were cleared to return we were able to get everyone fed and settled in. That night we all slept very well.

Larisa's parents did not work and they tried to help us with babysitting. Our apartment was just across Golden Gate Park in the Sunset district, and every day Evelina was taken there for a long ride in her baby carriage. When Larisa and I had the time, we would join the walk. One day we strolled through a mysteriously sweet-smelling part of the park. Unbeknownst to us, there was a small grocery store nestled in the park in which we made our first gourmet discovery: the delicious ice cream sandwich "It's-It". We (especially Larisa) became totally obsessed with it, and each of our visits to the park would inevitably bring us to that store for our treat.

In San Francisco I tried Chinese food for the first time and loved it. We also found Russian food stores where, among other delicious things, I bought challah. I was thirty-six years old when I broke my first challah.

Our first visit to the dentist would be remembered not only by us, but also by the dentist and all of his staff. Let me back up a little. Just before leaving the Soviet Union, we were advised to take care of our teeth, since, as we were told, the dental service in America was ungodly expensive. Our Moscow dentist built three bridges in my mouth, and unloaded a good pound of lead to fill in my cavities.

After an oral examination in the San Francisco office, the dentist discovered almost 30 cavities in my mouth and approximately the same number in Larisa's! After he took care of our teeth, I learned one thing quickly: the dental service in the United States was much better and more advanced than it was in Russia.

Meanwhile I started to explore the local artistic scene. Since the violin I brought from Russia was not of good quality and far below American standards, about a year after our arrival to San Francisco my friends arranged for me to borrow a violin. It was presented to me as Italian and it had much better sound than mine. I liked that fiddle very much. I played concerts and auditions on that violin, and promised myself that if I won the audition, I would do everything to buy it. (This story comes later.)

I made my first money playing recitals in big mansions, where I was also able to create some connections. Another friend of mine had arranged for me to work at the Hebrew Academy, where I was supposed to teach kids Jewish songs in Hebrew. I could not understand a word in Hebrew, but that wasn't a problem since the director of the Academy liked me very much. In fact, one day he even gave me a fancy suit which had earlier belonged to his son. The suit was a bit small, especially in the sleeves, but the quality of the wool was excellent.

Another challenging adventure presented itself. Larisa and I were asked to play Mozart's *Marriage of Figaro* with the Pocket Opera. The word 'pocket' referred to the tiny budget of the group, which was also reflected in the size of the orchestra. Strings were represented by a quartet in which I played first violin and Larisa played second. The "orchestra" was reinforced by a few winds and timpani. I believe that the whole orchestra consisted of no more than nine people. (Yes, there were singers too! They weren't able to cut the cast without ruining the opera's story line, so there were thirteen singers in all.) It was quite fun to play solos all the time, but we couldn't afford to miss a note (accidently) or relax a bit (intentionally) in that entire three hour opera packed with thousands of notes. We were exhausted, but the audience loved it.

The first apartment we rented was quite small: a one-bedroom for five people including newcomer Evelina, but we managed to invite a couple of new friends to our place for a party. We wanted to impress them (particularly our new American friends) with the mysteries of Russian-Jewish cuisine. Among other delicious dishes, we served a beet salad with garlic, crushed nuts and mayonnaise. It was a tasty salad, and we ate it quite often, but for our guests it was a new dish. They loved it, and ate all of it. As I learned much later, the next morning one of our guests almost fainted when she went to the bathroom and discovered that her urine was bright red. She made an immediate appointment with her doctor, who ordered extensive tests just to discover that everything was all right. The beets had done their job well. Since then, every time we have American friends over, I always warn them about the colorful side effects of beet salad, and also tell them this story. By the way, we remain very good friends with that beet-loving person.

25 · First Car

For the second time in my life, I felt the trembling of a building: the earthquake came early in the morning. We slept so deeply that nobody had the energy to wake up. We thought it was a dream, but that morning the same dream appeared to all residents of San Francisco. The quake did not last long, and caused almost no damage. It was an aftershock, following a major earthquake that had shaken California a few months earlier, causing substantial damage. I really hated earthquakes, and decided to get out of California to a safer place. Ironically, my first full-time job would be in Seattle, which is seismically just as dangerous as San Francisco, but I did not know that yet. Meanwhile, I continued to practice diligently every free minute I had.

Since we had only one violin for the two of us, Larisa would pick up the violin any time I stopped practicing and commence her routine: scales, etudes, concertos, and orchestral excerpts. We were starting to get more job offers from local orchestras, but they were spread out all over the Bay Area, and we needed a car.

Our first car was a beauty: dark blue with leather seats. It was roomy and comfortable, and I imagined it bouncing over bumps in the road like a king's carriage. We loved our Ford LTD. It cost us $900, and we couldn't have cared less how many miles were on it! Gas was 90 cents a gallon, and for the year and a half we stayed in San Francisco, the Ford served us very well, never once stalling.

Our first car in America

26 · Zoya and Leon

One day a lady knocked on the door of our apartment, and introduced herself as Zoya Leybin. I had already heard about this famous Russian violinist who played with the San Francisco Symphony. She asked about my plans, and I told her I was practicing all the time in preparation for playing auditions. She was a practical woman, and explained that the Bay Area was flooded with musicians, so it was nearly impossible to get a job playing the fiddle. She suggested that I change professions right away, and sign up for computer programming courses. Nearby Silicon Valley was experiencing an unprecedented boom in its economy, driven by the computer business. She said that in six months I could have a steady salary of $60,000. For me, that mirage of a number was equivalent to something equally abstract, like a million dollars.

When she left, my thoughts were all mixed up. I could not practice, and went for a walk. I wandered around the park, feeling detached from reality. People were friendly, but I felt that they were strangers, and did not care about me or anything else. I knew nothing about computers, and could not imagine changing my profession from one in which I had been successful all my life to something so alien. This was a dark day in my life.

A few days later a friend of mine introduced me to another violinist who played with the San Francisco Opera. He was a guy approximately my age, and soon became my close friend and supporter. Leon Igudesman came to our apartment, looked around, and said that he would come back in half an hour. We had no idea why he left that quickly. Half an hour later, true to his word, he returned with two huge packages full of delicatessen food. The most delicious item was a fresh French baguette sticking out of the paper bag. We had not enough words to thank him. I told Leon our story, including the recent visit of Zoya. He became agitated. "Don't listen to her! She says this to every new violinist coming from Russia. She does not want to have any competition. Don't even think of dropping the violin! Practice!"

This was so encouraging that I doubled my practice hours. Leon gave me a few valuable pointers on how to practice, and how to play auditions. This was a totally new experience to me and an entirely new approach to violin playing. I played well, but that was not enough to get a job in an American orchestra. I needed more precision in everything: intonation, rhythm, phrasing, quality of sound. It is interesting that just a few months later, the same Zoya Leybin would offer me free lessons in preparation for orchestra auditions, and would actually be responsible for my getting a position with the Seattle Symphony Orchestra. Looking back, my guess is that on her first visit to me she may have just been testing my devotion to the violin.

Meanwhile, our family became very close to Leon's. His wife Natasha played viola in the same orchestra, and they had a daughter just a bit older than Eva. We spent a lot of time together, playing duos with Leon. One time the San Francisco Opera was on lockout, and Leon called me to bring my violin. We went to Fisherman's Wharf, opened our cases, and started to play. That day we made over $200 at the popular tourist destination, and divided the money evenly. It was my first big catch! Leon made some arrangements and we went to play at the Lake Tahoe Music Festival. Beside the fact that I made some money, I had an opportunity to play with the best local musicians, some of whom were members of the San Francisco Symphony. Jeremy Cohen, a brilliant violinist and my friend who also worked as a contractor for recordings, invited me to play on the soundtrack of *The Terminator*. I still love that movie.

With Leon Igudesman at the Lake Tahoe Music Festival

Leon took me to garage and estate sales. Our trips became exciting weekly treasure hunts. I had never seen such a variety of people's stuff; most of it was actually junk. I learned the basics about auctions. I was introduced to a few local violin dealers, and started to fill in the gaps in my education about violins and bows. Foggy San Francisco did not seem to me that foggy since we were very busy, and our lives were starting to brighten.

The small ball of snow had begun its descent down a large hill; Larisa and I were getting more and more jobs. I was invited to play with the San Francisco String Quartet. That was a big step up for me as it meant that great local musicians recognized me as their equal. At some point I was invited to play as the Associate Concertmaster of the Oakland Symphony, but that was only a part-time job. I needed to support my family. I needed to find a steady income.

27 · Auditions

Auditions are difficult and stressful, but if you are well pre-pared, they can open doors to great opportunities. I started to look for audition opportunities. The first one for the San Francisco Symphony was a total disaster. At least two dozen violinists were packed into one room practicing all of the most notoriously diffi-cult passages, many of them playing from memory. I felt that all of these players were so much better than I, and they probably were. I did not advance to the second round.

An audition for the Sacramento Symphony did get me to the second round, and then I played another one for the San Francisco Opera. I did not get hired, but something good did come of it. After the audition, I was called to play an onstage part for Verdi's opera, *The Masked Ball*. That was the best gig I'd had so far; even the contracted orchestra musicians were envious of me. I only had to play for ten minutes onstage but was paid for the whole show. Of course, I had to come half an hour earlier to change into the funny 19th century costume and get my face powdered. After the dress rehearsal, the production director ran backstage in horror: I had played onstage in my wig but with my own dark beard. He ex-plained that it was not possible for the musician to have a beard for the show, and asked me to shave it. I had no problem with it, since I usually shaved it off from time to time anyway.

Before...   *...and after*
('Masked Ball' at San Francisco Opera)

Then somebody told me about the openings in the Seattle Symphony. Seattle musicians had broken away from the American

Federation of Musicians, a very powerful national union, in 1988, and created their own union. There were serious reasons for this development. The disadvantage for those who wanted to audition was that the Seattle Symphony could not advertise its openings in the musicians' paper, which belonged to AFM. News of Seattle auditions came only by word of mouth. I contacted the Seattle Symphony manager Ron Simon, and he told me how I could apply.

One day Leon Igudesman called me in great excitement, practically yelling into the phone. "Come to the opera rehearsal tomorrow at 1 p.m.! Jerry will be conducting, and I will introduce you to him."

"Who is Jerry?" I asked.

"Jerry Schwarz is the Music Director of the Seattle Symphony."

Nervous, I arrived at exactly the time I was told to watch Schwarz work with the orchestra in rehearsal. At 1 p.m. it was over, and the conductor was still exhilarated from the rehearsal. Leon approached him and introduced me.

"In what position did you play with the Moscow Symphony?" he asked.

"I played as Assistant Principal Second Violin."

"Oh, I have exactly the same opening in my orchestra," Jerry said. I smiled upon hearing this, but I wasn't sure how to react to his comment. Did this mean he might consider me for the Seattle position?

"Call me tomorrow in the afternoon. I want to hear you," Jerry added. Leon's face shone with satisfaction. I was struck by the tremendous opportunity, but a moment later realized that it was not going to happen. "I am sorry, but my flight to Seattle is tomorrow at 8 a.m. The first round of auditions starts in the afternoon," I said. Jerry shrugged his shoulders as if to say, "I gave you a chance."

The next morning I flew to Seattle, and Peter Kaman, a Seattle Symphony violinist who was Leon's friend, met me at the airport. He brought me to his apartment, and let me practice and stay there during my audition. I practiced 5-7 hours a day, with absolute concentration and in the way Zoya had taught me. Peter was mesmerized by my discipline, and expressed his admiration repeatedly. I learned that more than 200 people had applied for four positions, and only 40 were allowed to play a live audition. I passed the first two rounds (done behind a screen), and advanced to the finals. This was already miracle enough for me. I was told that only five players, including myself, had advanced to the final round, and I thought I might have a chance. There were five candidates for four positions.

The third round was held without the screen, and the Music Director was present. Before each round, those auditioning had to draw a number to determine the order in which they would be playing. Then I saw more than five people in the room going to draw a number. As somebody explained to me later, the Music Director had the right to directly invite to the finals anyone he had previously auditioned in private and who was qualified enough, according to his standards. So there were eight people now. I got the feeling that this was the end for me. There was nothing to lose; I just went on stage and played my best.

After the committee discussion, Jerry called each player into his room one by one. He had the final word on giving the job to the candidate, no matter what the committee had decided. The committee just needed to qualify the player with their stamp of approval in order for the musician to advance further in the process of the Music Director's final decision.

Jerry was sitting in an armchair like a king. To complete the picture of the power he radiated, I would have added a cigar to his right hand (as I learned later, he did smoke cigars, though not at that moment). He said, "Michael, I decided to grant you the highest position available: Assistant Principal Second Violin. Congratulations! I guess that you know the repertoire well. Bravo!"

I don't really remember how I responded; my head was foggy. I just said, "Thank you." So much effort, so much arduous practice and preparation – and what an exciting reward! I was the only player who had passed through all three rounds and got the job. The other three violinists were those invited to the finals, and I was very proud to have gotten my position in an honest way, not owing anybody anything for it.

The next thing I remember was dialing the number of our apartment in San Francisco. Larisa picked up the phone. "I hope you will like Seattle," I said.

28 · Fake Italian

I flew back to San Francisco, rented a U-Haul, and put the stuff that we had managed to accumulate from the last 14 months in the truck. Evelina went into her car seat, and we departed for a new life in Seattle. (I did not forget to return the violin I had been borrowing, with gratitude, to its owner.) We rushed to Seattle because right after the audition I got an offer to play with the Seattle Opera for a summer production of Wagner's spectacular four-opera cycle, *Der Ring des Nibelungen*. It was a great offer and I was so excited to finally have a real full-time job! I played in the first violin section for those long and enormously difficult operas. Since I had never played anything from *The Ring* before, it was a huge amount of music to practice: hundreds of pages with millions of notes. Coming home after the 4 to 6-hour shows, my back was on fire. I had to lie on ice for half an hour to numb the pain.

I remembered the promise I gave to myself to buy the violin that had helped me win the audition. Sometime later I called the owner asking if he might change his mind and sell me the violin (at first he had absolutely refused to sell it). To my sincere surprise, he said yes. The violin was shipped to Seattle for certification. The owner told me that the violin was made almost 200 years ago by an Italian master, and his asking price was $50,000. After a thorough examination by a couple of local violin dealers I was told that in their opinion, the violin was made by a Czech master no more than 100 years ago. The instrument also had the wrong dimensions, which would require the player to make a serious effort to play in tune. It's amazing how I managed to adapt to these wrong dimensions during the couple of months I had the violin in my hands. (I must have played my Seattle audition in tune; otherwise I would not have gotten the job!) "What might be the price?" I asked a dealer.

"Not more than $2,500. $3,000 if you really like it."

I was stunned. No less surprised was the owner when I told him the news. He probably did not believe the dealers, absolutely refused to negotiate, and with regret I sent the violin back.

29 · The Apartment

Peter was kind enough to rent us a one-bedroom apartment in Seattle's Queen Anne neighborhood. It was close to the Opera House where the Seattle Symphony practiced and performed. After Bay Area traffic, the 10-minute drive to work was paradise. We often had two rehearsals a day with a 90-minute break in between, and I had enough time to drive home, have lunch, and kiss my girls. Peter also helped me open my bank account and apply for my first credit card. Larisa was busy with Evelina. Everything was going very well, and life was rosy.

One day, I was on my way back from opera rehearsal, and on the way home I decided to stop by the store for some groceries. When I came home and opened the door to our apartment I sensed a tension. Larisa was nervous and upset, and told me what had happened. Peter, who had also played that rehearsal with me, had come straight home, grabbed his cute little dog, and went for a walk. The apartment he lived in with his wife was just half a block from ours. Larisa was also taking a walk with Evelina in her stroller and saw what had happened from a distance. I guess Peter, excited as always, wanted to chat and share his boiling antipathy toward the opera conductor (Peter could not stand authority). He had come up to our apartment building, buzzed the doorbell, and, as we were both out, nobody answered. He buzzed again, and instead of us the building manager came out. She was just on her way out and the timing could not have been worse.

I learned what had happened from Peter. The manager angrily said that dogs were not allowed in the building. Peter asked why she was addressing him in that tone, and that he was not planning to enter the premises with the dog. She grew agitated and asked him to leave. He stubbornly responded that it wasn't prohibited to stay with a dog at the door outside of the building. She became angry and kicked the dog. Now it was Peter's turn to protect his baby and he hit the manager back. Larisa saw it happen at a distance, but she was too far away to know exactly what had happened.

The following events unfolded with cosmic speed. The manager ran away, and a few minutes later the police arrived. They handcuffed Peter and took him to the police station. He was soon released, but the manager had put a brace on her arm, claiming that Peter had broken it. To make the story short: the case was taken to court, and Peter told Larisa that if she did not tell the court that the manager had hit the dog first, he might go to prison.

Larisa testified to that effect, but that only triggered more trouble. One day I discovered that our recently purchased Toyota Corolla, which we always parked in the gated building garage, had been keyed. I reported this to the police, explaining what had preceded the incident, but there was no evidence, and the manager, who had quickly recovered from her "broken" arm, smiled devilishly each time we met.

One night Larisa went to work, and I had a free evening. I stayed home with Evelina. It was late in the evening and I was giving my daughter a bath when I heard a loud knock at the door. I rushed to the door, opened it, but nobody was there. The manager obviously wanted to make us uncomfortable and kick us out. It was impossible to stay in such a hostile environment, especially with a child. We had to find a new place, and we felt ready for our own house.

30 · Our American Dream

Do you know how many houses we looked at before we found the one that realized our American dream? More than 80. We liked our house right away even though it smelled quite bad; the previous owner had been a heavy smoker. At the time, the real estate market was not too hot, and the seller was flexible with the price. The house was ours! It took a long time, however, to make it feel like home. We were busy at work all day long, and at night we tried to rip the smelly wallpaper off the walls. It seemed that it was glued with super glue. Slowly we cleaned up the house, bought new furniture, and finished the basement for our own practicing and for a place to teach our students.

There was a flood of students right away. Word had spread about two Russian violinists from Moscow, and we grew incredibly busy. Students' cars could hardly move in our driveway, which we shared with two other neighbors, and this caused discontent on the part of one of the neighbors. He was not accustomed to seeing so many cars coming in and out during the day, since the previous owner had been an elderly man who lived alone.

One day I heard a ring at the front door. The man introduced himself as a representative of the City License department. He told me that our neighbor had filed a complaint about the increased traffic in our driveway. As evidence, that neighbor had even supplied photographs of the students' cars and their license plates. There was not any limit on traffic of course, but I did not know that we had to get a license from the city in order to operate our own business. The next day I obtained a license for our teaching business and even got the name for it: Miropolsky School of Violin. Now we were fully licensed business people!

I had talented students and not-so-talented students, lazy ones and hardworking ones, children and adults. Along with the necessary technical and musical skills, I taught my students to think independently, find their own way, not be afraid to experiment, learn how to take responsibility for their actions, and eventually become their own teachers with the ability to pass their skills on to the next generation.

My students helped me rediscover myself through teaching, to become a better violinist and musician. Thanks to teaching, I learned to be imaginative and patient, and I met so many wonderful people. I think I inherited the talent for teaching from my father, and also acquired the knowledge from my teachers, to whom I am eternally grateful.

31 · Movie Recordings

In the beginning of the 1990s, Seattle suddenly became a mecca for the movie recording business. Many Hollywood composers rushed to Seattle to record soundtracks for their movies. The reason was simple: Seattle musicians had created their own union, and they did not want to be told by the American Federation of Musicians and its big bosses what and when to record. Why did Hollywood come to Seattle? If the same recordings had taken place in Los Angeles, musicians who were members of the AFM would be paid more than $200 per hour, plus lifetime royalties. Seattle musicians agreed to do the same job for just $55 per hour and without any royalties. The LA local union was unhappy to be losing jobs, but could not do anything about it.

We musicians got an enormous amount of work. On some of our days "off" we worked 10 hours, and often managed to come to recording sessions between Seattle Symphony Orchestra schedules. We recorded music for hundreds of movies, and later for computer games as well. Recordings took place mostly at the Bastyr University Chapel with its naturally wonderful acoustics, but unfortunately without any ventilation or air conditioning. In summertime it was especially hard to record without fresh air, since all the doors and windows had to be shut to prevent any incoming sounds from interfering with the recording.

Many talented movie composers came to Seattle, and they were happy with the high quality of the recordings we were making. Michael Kamen was one of the most brilliant composers of his generation and left strong memories in our hearts. He was a real artist. To start with, he was a man without any strict sense of time. Our recording sessions usually started at 10 a.m. In the best-case scenario, by 10:30 a.m. his huge limousine would arrive at the front door of the Bastyr Chapel. Sporting a long, dark coat, he would spend another 10-15 minutes hugging and kissing his beautiful girlfriend. We had no idea who she was.

Working with Kamen was fun. He also conducted the recording sessions himself. He had a big talent and the musicians felt it right away. His music had life and imagination, and he always provided food for the musicians at the breaks. He knew that well-fed musicians played better. Then, when the project was over, he would throw the kind of party comparable to those of the Roman Empire. I had read about such parties in the history books. You also can see them depicted on the TV show *Rome*. Are you getting hungry? I am.

32 · Seattle Symphony Orchestra

My tenure with the Seattle Symphony began in 1991. Since then I have had the privilege of sharing the stage with extraordinary musicians: Mstislav Rostropovich, Van Cliburn, Luciano Pavarotti, Itzhak Perlman, Pinchas Zukerman, Lynn Harrell, Yo-Yo Ma, Marvin Hamlisch, Renée Fleming, and many others. I had the honor of playing a solo with the distinguished Jaime Laredo, and enjoyed the mastery of such visiting conductors as Kurt Mazur, Vassily Sinaisky, and Thomas Dausgaard. The Seattle Symphony does not travel much, but we have made several successful concert tours including two trips to New York. Carnegie Hall has wonderful acoustics indeed: very "alive" is how I would describe them. On one occasion, as a member of the string quartet I had the rare privilege of playing for President Bill Clinton when he was visiting Seattle. At some point when we were passing each other at a close distance, I noticed that the President was taller than I was.

At the beginning of my tenure with the Seattle Symphony Orchestra, my symphony colleagues and I formed a string quartet and named it "The Emerald String Quartet." As part of the Seattle Symphony's educational program, we made numerous presentations at schools in the state of Washington. The kids were adorable, and the most popular question posed to me was, "How much are you paid?" The five-year-olds were already interested in my family life. They also were very surprised to learn that the violin I played was made in 1845 (I may as well have said 30 BC) but inevitably followed up with a question about its worth.

I always liked to play in the symphony orchestra, and I would consider myself more of an orchestra musician than a chamber musician. I respect my colleagues who love to play in smaller ensembles: quartets, trios, or performing in duos. There is such intimate tenderness and beauty in chamber music. But I like to be a part of big drama and big, intense emotions. Only a symphony orchestra can provide these qualities and that level of excitement. For example, each time I play Ravel's *Bolero*, I am in ecstasy from its melody and pulsating rhythm, though the composer himself actually said, "There is no music in that piece." If that were true, audiences and musicians wouldn't be so crazy about it.

People often ask me who my favorite composer or my favorite piece of music is, and I cannot give them a straight answer. I simply don't have one. When I play Mozart, I am in love with Mozart; when I play Tchaikovsky, he becomes the greatest composer at that moment for me. One thing I know for sure is that music appeals first of all to our emotions, not to our brains, and if I don't feel that emotional connection, then to me, that piece is no good. I trust my intuition, and it hasn't yet led me astray when it comes to musical judgment.

I find it interesting that nobody has ever asked me the question, "How do you listen to music?" With regret, I have to admit that I cannot enjoy a musical piece the way most people do. From the first sound of the piece my ears and my brain start to analyze the music: "What piece is it? Who is the composer?" and after the initial analysis comes the next round: "What key is it written in? Which instrument is playing this tune? Why is the tempo so slow? Who is conducting and what orchestra can it be?" And so on and so on. Rarely can I strip off all these questions that appear automatically before me, and just relax and enjoy the piece. This is the other side of my education and my gift of perfect pitch.

When I signed my initial contract in 1991 with the Seattle Symphony, I also started to work for the Seattle Opera. I liked to play in the pit and had the opportunity to perform many wonderful operas (and, unfortunately, a few that were not so wonderful). Larisa was also often invited to play with the Seattle Opera as well as with the Seattle Symphony. She played with practically every local orchestra, also making a lot of recordings and teaching many students. With deep respect I watched how much energy and dedication she put into every project she worked on.

At the start of 1993, the Seattle Symphony went on tour to Florida. Larisa was also invited to play in the orchestra, and we had a lot of fun on the trip. In fact, we had so much fun that on August 3rd of the same year, our family welcomed a new little boy – Alex. He was also a premature baby, but was born with a lot of dark hair. At first he did not want to scream as all babies are supposed to do upon entering this world. But after a short reminder of his responsibility in the form of a ringing slap, he agreed to say his "hello."

With newborn Alex

When Evelina was born in San Francisco, the doctors said that right after the delivery Larisa had to put therapeutic ice on her stomach. After delivering Alex in Seattle, Larisa was told to use heat therapy. I could not imagine that in two different states they would use such opposite postpartum protocols. But you know what? Both worked! (I also remember when Yulia was born in Moscow, Alla and the baby were held at the hospital for a week without visitors, so I would talk to Alla standing under their room window and use some sort of sign language. Upon returning home no relatives or friends were allowed to see Yulia for a month, whereas here in America visitors for newborns were allowed from day one.)

In 1993 I had the pleasure of performing with the Chamber Music Society of Seattle under the direction of an outstanding oboist, Alex Klein. He later became principal oboe of the Chicago Symphony and received a Grammy Award for Best Instrumental Soloist Performance with Orchestra. For a couple of seasons I played as Concertmaster of the Northwest Sinfonietta, and performed with them as a soloist. I taught on the faculty of the University of Puget Sound, continued to give violin master classes, and made presentations there as a conductor as well.

I started to get recognized on the street and in the shopping malls. One day I was taking a bus in downtown Seattle to get to

Benaroya Hall. The bus driver saw me carrying my violin case and immediately struck up a conversation on the importance of J. S. Bach's influence on the following generations of composers. I was speechless; first at hearing such an unexpectedly intelligent lecture from the bus driver, and also because I felt that he knew much more than I on the topic. It was more of a monologue than a conversation, but I enjoyed it a lot. Once I was identified as a musician even on a Caribbean cruise thousands of miles away from Seattle. But the funniest encounter happened when I went for a swim in the Queen Anne pool. After my swim, I was taking a shower (sans swimsuit) when a man next to me (also sans swimsuit) turned to me and asked, "Aren't you Michael Miropolsky, and you play with the Seattle Symphony?"

33 · Orchestra People

For the majority of orchestra musicians, playing in a symphony orchestra is fun, because they have trained for this job all their lives in music school and in conservatories. But it's no secret that in every orchestra there are people who dislike their job. The audience can easily spot them by their dead appearance on the stage. These unhappy people ended up in the orchestra by a stroke of fate. During many years of school training they never imagined themselves ending up in the orchestra. In their dreams they would become the great soloists who would stand in front of that grey untalented mass of miserable orchestra musicians, and impress the world with their unsurpassable virtuosity and hypnotic solo artistry.

The fates played a bad joke on them and these players became a depressed addition to that grey and pitiful mass. Every day and every minute playing in the orchestra is a torture for them. They look upon every player in their section as a pathetic failure, and every conductor as an egomaniac. These unhappy people project their own failure onto everything around them. They despise their colleagues, conductors, and soloists. They hate the administration and the music they play. They hate their job. They don't realize that they hate themselves. Fortunately, relatively few symphony players are like that.

The next and largest category consists of players who in general like their job. Nobody is perfect and these people can be annoyed at times by the circumstances that accompany the job, such as the stand partner who misbehaves, smells bad, or misses notes. The most standard complaint is that there is too much work and not enough pay. These people will often criticize – but only moderately – the conductors, repertoire, management, and working conditions. Most of the time these players are satisfied with their job. They make up the core of the orchestra.

The final category contains a precious few players who accept all aspects of their job almost blindly and without critique. They are always happy, but one needs to have some powerful binoculars to spot them in the orchestra. They are the minority.

All these different players create an amazing mix of characters and temperaments; together they are a symphony orchestra. When it comes to a performance, everyone remembers their professional duty: to do their job as best they can, almost like soldiers in an army. The personal becomes secondary, and teamwork is primary. This quality becomes especially important when in front of the orchestra stands an untalented conductor. In such a case it is up to the musicians to save the concert if the conductor cannot do so. They must go ahead like the professionals they are, even if they are not getting any help from the podium. If this happens often, the musicians lose their enthusiasm.

On the contrary, when a great conductor comes, the orchestra becomes unrecognizable, even visually. Audiences will immediately see extra body motion from the musicians, their backs getting straighter, and their bodies at full attention. The players lift their eyes and one can see the spark in them. In such moments even "dead" musicians come back to life for a while, and the same Beethoven symphony they have played a hundred times sounds like never before. Such talented conductors have the innate ability to inspire musicians, and bring them along on an exciting musical journey. When such a transformation happens, all the musicians are happy, and so are the audiences and critics. The players give everything they have, and they will remember that concert for a long time to come.

34 · The Other Side of the Coin

There is not a professional symphony orchestra that would hire musicians without a college education, because in order to reach that high level of professionalism and be qualified for the job, one has to have at least 15 years of musical education under their belt. A musician's profession is one of the hardest to achieve. The pleasure and honor of calling music your profession comes with a high price. To start with, one needs to have exceptional musical talent. Talent of this requisite level is a rare thing. The discovery of such talent is followed by thousands of hours of practicing, while the repetitive motion places constant pressure on muscles and stress on nerves. I have known quite a few relatively young musicians who had to end their careers as orchestral players because of something called "overuse syndrome." In short, it means one has overworked the muscles of the hands or neck.

In an orchestra, violinists and violists sit in the most awkward position: the upper body twists to the right while heads twist to the left. That's how we play our instruments. The worst part for us is that this position hardly changes, particularly when we have to play slow notes or repetitive rhythm figurations on one of the low strings for an extended period of time. Second violins and violas suffer the most, since many orchestra parts are written that way for them. Holding the right elbow in an elevated position while twisting the left hand can cause one to feel numbness or a sharp pain in the middle or upper back within several seconds. If the player does not change position and allow the stiff muscles to release, the pain might eventually become chronic. Unfortunately, orchestra musicians don't have the luxury of controlling when they can relax their muscles. The music must go on.

When it comes to medical professionals, chiropractors and massage therapists are a musician's best friend. Among others, cellists and double bass players have a much more natural position while playing compared to their violin and viola playing colleagues. This does not mean, however, that they don't experience physical problems associated with their profession. All instrumentalists have their own complaints: for woodwind and brass players, the problems relate mostly to the lips and facial muscles; for percussionists, it is their wrists.

Another unpleasant part of the musical profession is stage fright. This phenomenon does not usually afflict orchestra section players, who work as a team and cover each other's back while playing the same melodic or rhythmic line. However, I have known a few musicians who were so afraid of the conductor, that even sitting in the last stand of the violins made them so nervous that they had to take medication to calm their nerves. The orchestra principal players, whose parts are much more exposed than those of section players, know what it means to be nervous and how to cope with their anxiety.

Conductors tend to deal much better with stage anxiety. For them, the nervousness often ends the moment the conducting starts. The worst possible technical mistake that a conductor can make is to give the wrong cue, but most musicians are trained enough that they will not react to such an error. Orchestra players always count the bars and know their entrances well. Being in the state of music creation pushes the fear away, so that the conductor can remain focused and in control throughout the performance.

Concert soloists have a very different relationship with stage fright. Most of them are pretty good at handling this vulnerability; otherwise, they would not be able to play even a few notes in front of an audience, but others deal with such situations in rather unusual ways. One famous Russian pianist, Oleg Bochniakovich, panicked whenever he approached the stage. He would pay the stage director five rubles each time he played a concert so the stage director would open the door, literally push him onstage, and quickly close the door behind him. Once on stage there was no turning back, so Bochniakovich would have no choice but to proceed toward the piano. Then, as he sat before his instrument, his fear would completely evaporate. He would play a beautiful recital and never experienced any stage fright while he played. Another famous violinist used to drink a glass of cognac just before a concert, a habit that would make any other player unable to play in tune. Not only would this man play everything with the purest intonation, he also never failed to impress the audience with an altogether stunning performance.

Another interesting aspect of performance anxiety is the physiological relationship between the musicians and the audience. Some famous concert soloists admit that in order for them to create beautiful music the presence of the audience is not at all necessary (e.g., pianist Sviatoslav Richter). Conversely, some artists ask to keep the lights on or half dimmed so that they can see the audience, whose presence inspires them to play. Some are unable to record well in the studio if their only audience is a sole, indifferent microphone. Some cannot play in front of an audience at all, but are able to make phenomenal recordings in the studio with only the microphone for company (e.g., Glenn Gould).

Orchestra musicians cannot afford to be so picky. We like the audience and we need the audience. We cannot stand to see the concert hall half empty. In this case the saying about the optimist who sees the glass half-full does not apply. When the hall is half full, it's half empty! But this does not mean that we are pessimists. We just try to play better, with more energy and inspiration, and hope for a full house the next time around.

35 · Citizenship

1995 was an especially exciting year for our family. Five years had passed since we had arrived in the "land of our dreams," and Larisa and I were in the midst of preparing for the naturalization test. We were nervous, probably like all other immigrants who were about to be granted their American citizenship. We studied day and night, and successfully passed the test. In a big room with a couple hundred other men and women we took the Naturalization Oath and wept tears of happiness. It was a tremendous and unforgettable day in our lives.

Coming back home from the festive ceremony, we found a message on our answering machine from my Seattle Symphony colleague, Bruce Bailey. He said that we had an important meeting that night at 7 p.m., and we should be dressed nicely and arrange for a babysitter. We called the babysitter. We had absolutely no idea what was going on.

A few minutes before 7 p.m., Bruce knocked on our door. He was a bit short of breath (our steep driveway made everyone out of breath), and asked us to follow him. We followed him down the driveway. "Where are we going?" I was so curious. "Just follow me," said Bruce. We went around the block and saw his wife Mariel and Vince Comer. I had worked with these guys at the Seattle Symphony for a few years already, and we had become friends. As the Emerald String Quartet we had played a number of concerts and also performed at Seattle schools.

They were dressed very nicely, and stood beside a huge limousine. "Hello, guys," they greeted us. "Please get in." We were intrigued since we had never been inside a limo, and found it spacious and comfortable. "What's going on?" I was anxious and kept asking questions. "Michael, just relax. We will show you the best of Seattle." Larisa and I could not say that in our four years of living in Seattle we knew the city well; we worked a lot and spent the rest of the time with our kids.

We took an hour-long tour around Seattle with its beautiful downtown, parks, boulevards, and then arrived at a restaurant called Kasper's. We did not know about the existence of that fine restaurant on the top of Queen Anne hill. The dinner was superb, and it was such a wonderful evening that our friends had arranged for us. Glasses of champagne were raised for the new citizens of the United States of America, and a year later, for the first time, we voted for the President of the United States.

Proud to finally be American citizens!

Interlude: What is Success?

Along with millions of other immigrants, we came to America with our dreams. Most immigrants I know came to this country with the dream of finding success. But how can one measure success? Getting rich, taking an important position in a company, or in my case – having a good job in the orchestra, and being able to conduct one? All of the above looks like success to me. Or maybe it's not that tangible, and success is really about finding balance in life, peace in one's soul, or finding God.

Is the man who has become a millionaire (or, in these days, a billionaire) and CEO of a new tech company more successful than a mother who has raised three kids, helping them to get a college education, and teaching them how to become good parents themselves?

Success as I understand it is to find deep inside you something that requires realization, and then to find a way to bring it to life. It had better be something constructive, and this is the only way to the highest freedom and happiness we all search for. In this country we all have opportunities to find this highest freedom. Needless to say, this was not possible back in Russia.

Each of us has many talents. Musical gifts are very special talents, but how many musicians are unhappy while being blessed with that rare gift, just because they haven't found what is real inside of them? Until we can make such a discovery, we cannot be happy.

36 · Seattle Conservatory of Music

During my first years in Seattle, I also conducted the orchestra at Northwest School, founded the Jewish Community Center Chamber Orchestra, and in 1997, accepted an invitation from Margaret Pressley, a very well-known violin teacher in the area, to create a student orchestra at the newly opened Seattle Conservatory of Music. The best students joined that orchestra which I named "The Young Virtuosi Chamber Orchestra." I also started a second student orchestra where we sight read a new symphonic piece at every rehearsal. It helped the students expand their symphonic repertoire and improve their ability to sight read, which is one of the most important qualities one needs to have in order to get a job with a symphony orchestra. These young men and women really were virtuosi, and we enjoyed six wonderful years of music making, even recording a brilliant CD, until the program ended for financial reasons. At that time, after 9/11, many artistic organizations in America experienced financial trouble due to the economic downturn, and even some very solid symphony orchestras had to undergo bankruptcy.

Seattle Conservatory of Music Young Virtuosi Chamber Orchestra

I keep on the wall the following framed letter "To the Best Maestro" with all of the students' signatures and a pack of their letters to me. I cannot resist quoting a few of them:

"Dear Mr. Miropolsky,

... You are a fabulous conductor, and not to mention a fabulous violinist/musician."

"You are the best conductor that I have ever had the opportunity to play for. You have formed the SCM Young Virtuosi into the best student music group on the West Coast...and I will never forget the excitement I had when I joined the SCM orchestra. It was one of the best musical things that ever happened to me."

"I have great respect for you and your passion for excellence! You are honest and upfront (don't ever stop being upfront)! And the thing I like best about you is your discipline. More students need to have disciplined and responsible role models like you. Thank you for treating me like a professional and most of all for being honest with me."

"...None of us is perfect and you never penalize for that! I have never felt more pressure than I could handle to come and play here. I also love being able to laugh here. And you are not a slave driver. Thank you for being such a great conductor!"

"This orchestra was a truly inspiring experience. I came here with an interest in classical music that has now evolved into a passion for it. Your peaceful attitude and conducting created both an atmosphere of learning, but also of enjoyment. Thank you."

"I have loved having you as a conductor at Young Virtuosi. I think however, that your gift of singing will be most deeply felt, particularly when a flautist is absent. Many times I have heard a high note seeming to come from nowhere only to find it to be emitting from your throat. You have the most impressive range; the highest I have ever heard. I will miss your sense of humor a lot. Your ability to deliver jokes is incredible – you always deliver them straight..."

"I really had a lot of fun playing in this wonderful group with a wonder-full CONDUCTOR! I just thank God that I met you as a conductor. God bless you. I will miss you. P.S. I love your Russian accent!!"

And this one from a parent:

"Dear Michael,

I have felt it a rare treat to be present at many rehearsals to see you working with the students, breathing life into the compositions, coaching different sections with intelligence, enthusiasm and tact. You have molded beauty from what, at times, were very unskilled beginnings in our students. You have taught the students how to get in touch with their own muse, how to know and get in touch with the music. This is wonderful. Watching you conduct with vigor, passion and bold confidence is as enjoyable as the delightful musical program which is the inevitable result of all the weeks of rehearsals. Thank you for all you have done for our "Young Virtuosi!"

37 · Seattle Violin Virtuosi

I felt very comfortable in my position as Assistant Principal with the Seattle Symphony, also serving as Principal for almost half of the season. However, after a few years I started to feel that I was not as fully satisfied with the orchestra playing as I had been before, and felt the need to add something more to my musical life. I came to a crossroads where I wanted to create something on my own.

A brilliant idea came to mind. Back in Moscow I had attended concerts of the wonderful Violin Ensemble of the Bolshoi Theatre. It consisted of 18 violins and a piano accompaniment. Yuri Reentovich, one of the concertmasters of the orchestra, was founder and leader of the group. Their programs consisted of the most brilliant miniatures from the opera, choral, symphony, and instrumental repertoires. The ensemble even got a nickname: "A Big Violin of the Bolshoi." And really, when they played in unison it sounded like a single big violin with a huge tone, and when they played pieces arranged for three or four voices they sounded like a violin orchestra. That ensemble was very popular in Russia, and it was a tradition in the music schools to have a violin ensemble. Even in Frunze the music school had one.

This idea totally occupied my mind. In Seattle and other cities in America I had not heard of such an ensemble. A year before that, I had tried a couple of the pieces with my students at the Seattle Conservatory of Music, and that is where I got the feeling that this concept could grow into a concert performance. I started to work from scratch. There was no music available, no money, nothing except my enthusiasm, bordering on obsession. With great luck, one of the Seattle Symphony donors, Sam Rubinstein, agreed to sponsor the first concert. I hired 11 of the best available violinists, most of them from the Seattle Symphony. Victoria Bogdashevskaya (and later Irina Akhrin) became the ensemble's exquisite pianists. I reserved the Recital Hall at Benaroya Hall and started rehearsing.

It was exciting but hard work, since everything I did, I did for the first time. I found the music, searched through all possible catalogues, contacted my colleagues in Russia, Germany, England, and Israel, as well as arranging some of the music myself. I spent nights

writing out parts from the scores by hand for the musicians, design-
ing the layout of the program, contacting music critics, selecting
and ordering beautiful dark blue dresses for the women. With the
help of a lawyer who agreed to work pro bono for us, I created the
Seattle Virtuosi Foundation. I recruited the Board of Directors of
the Foundation (who later did all the fundraising), designed stationary, drew up contracts for musicians and concert venues, paid
bills, kept up business correspondence, and found a company that
would make our CD (we recorded the entire CD *On Wings of Song*
in just one three hour session!).

The Seattle Violin Virtuosi on stage at Benaroya Hall

I prepared talks to give to the audience, which they loved.
Since it worked so well, I later used this practice with all the other
orchestras I conducted. I found that it erased the barrier between
the performers and the audience, making audiences feel like they
were a part of the show. I worked on many other things during that
preconcert period, not to mention constantly practicing my own
parts (since I would be standing in the middle of the ensemble and
lead it by playing violin). Looking back, I am amazed at how much
I learned and how many new qualities I discovered within myself
during that exciting time of creation. We really don't know what we
are capable of until we try! My colleagues were also thrilled with

the unique idea of the Seattle Violin Virtuosi. They were very supportive and gave it their all.

At our inaugural concert, we presented eighteen adorable miniatures, including Anderson's *Fiddle Faddle*, Diniku's *Hora Staccato*, Khachaturian's *Sabre Dance*, and Mendelssohn's *On Wings of Song* (which became the title of the CD). The concert was sold out and an absolute success. We got great reviews from the critics. Seattle Times music critic Melinda Bargreen called the ensemble "The best of both musical worlds: Russian tradition and American excellence." I became very inspired with such a fantastic start, and began to plan our next concerts. Later I made a few more recordings with this group, some of them released on the *Ambassador* label. We accumulated almost 200 pieces in our repertoire. It was a wonderful time of creation. My life took on a new level of meaning.

Three years after founding the Seattle Violin Virtuosi, I started the Seattle Chamber Orchestra with the same violinists, adding violas, cellos, and a bass. I was lucky to lead these exceptional musicians who trusted me and followed me in this endeavor. We also recorded CDs with the Chamber Orchestra. Along with Tchaikovsky's *Elegy for Strings,* I consider our rendition of Shostakovich's tragic Chamber Symphony, an arrangement for the orchestra of his Eighth String Quartet, to be one of our most successful recordings.

38 · Cascade Symphony Orchestra

It was not that early on a Saturday morning, but still quite un-usual that someone would call at 9 a.m. on a weekend. The kids were still asleep, and we had allowed ourselves to sleep in a bit longer after an usually exhausting week. I picked up the phone ex-pecting a telemarketing call. First there was silence for a couple of seconds, typical for the advertising calls, and then a man asked if he could speak to Michael Miropolsky. My first thought was, "This time they actually learned how to pronounce my name correctly!" (At some point I wanted to compile a list of the misspelled and mispronounced variances of my last name. Even now I receive cor-respondence with new variations on my name. Here are a few of my favorites: Miropsky, Maropolsky, Mirski, Moripolsky, Mira-piski. It's like a game: who can twist this long surname in the most colorful way?) "Speaking," I said. "My name is..." I could not un-derstand the name. "One more word and I will hang up," I thought to myself. The man continued his obviously prepared speech, and I was very glad that I did not hang up. He said that he represented the Cascade Symphony Orchestra, and that they were looking for a substitute conductor for one program.

"Are you available on Monday nights?" he asked.

"Actually, yes," I said. "That is my only day and night off from the Seattle Symphony."

"Would you be interested in conducting a program with us?"

I had heard a bit about the orchestra, but did not follow the news, otherwise I would have known that the previous conductor had almost ruined that fine volunteer orchestra and brought it to bankruptcy. To pay the bills, the conductor, without consulting the board first, sold the orchestra's entire music library, as well as their music stands and all other orchestra equipment accumulated dur-ing the 40 years of the orchestra's existence. The orchestra players had been so disgusted with this conductor that they had withdrawn from the Cascade Symphony and formed a new orchestra, which they called the Classic Cascade Symphony. The orchestra was mi-raculously able to come back, taking back the Cascade Symphony name, and was auditioning potential candidates for a new music director. As I learned later, I was not on that list, and the only reason I was called was because one of the already scheduled candidates had a conflict and asked that his performance be postponed. The orchestra granted his request.

"Yes, I would be interested," I said.

"Then we would like to schedule an interview with you."

There were four or five people in the room, and they asked me all types of questions. This one was the most memorable: "Would you show us how you conduct?"

"What do you mean, how I conduct?" I lifted my right hand and showed the basic pattern in four-four time.

"We can see the beat!" they exclaimed, and seeing my surprise, explained that they could not decipher the previous conductor's beat. I found this both funny and very unfortunate. I got the job.

For the main piece of the Cascade program I chose Tchaikovsky's Symphony *Pathetique*. I love this symphony, and decided to take a double risk: making my first appearance with the orchestra with such deeply sorrowful music, and also conducting this symphony for the first time. I started studying the score.

Our family returned to the United States after a long European trip on September 10, 2001, just a day before my first rehearsal with the orchestra. Our last stop before departing to Seattle was Washington, DC. The next morning the whole world was shaken by the unimaginable terrorist attack on the Twin Towers in New York. People could not believe such a horrible act had occurred, and on a personal level we realized how lucky we had been to go through Washington, DC just a few hours before the tragedy happened.

At the rehearsal, even though we all were horrified by the fall of the World Trade Center and frightened by the total uncertainty of what the next day might bring, I was overwhelmed by the positive attitude of the musicians and their desire to play as best they could. The whole atmosphere was so different than in the professional orchestras in which I had played. The musicians smiled eagerly at me instead of glancing at their watches every few minutes, showing their total readiness to follow my directions. The rehearsal started at 7:30 p.m. with a 15-minute intermission, and was scheduled to run till 10 p.m.

I knew from my own orchestra experience that no matter how

good the conductor might be, the musicians would be happy if they were allowed to go home 5-10 minutes early. At seven minutes till 10 p.m. I stopped the rehearsal and said, "Thank you very much. We had a good rehearsal." There was no reaction from the musicians. I looked at people and they looked back at me in silence. I did not understand what was going on. With a questioning look in my eyes I turned to the concertmaster, and she quietly said, "We have another seven minutes."

I felt tears well up in my eyes. Never before had I heard of musicians choosing to practice right through to the last second of the designated rehearsal time. We finished the rehearsal at 10 p.m. sharp. After the second rehearsal, I was collecting my scores and noticed that a few people came to the podium. I recognized them from my interview. "Michael," they said, "please do not take any other jobs on Monday evenings. We want you to be our Music Director."

I was stunned. "Wait a minute. How about the other conductors that should work with you after my program? And what about that man who was supposed to conduct this program and whose performance was postponed for a later time?"

"Don't worry; we will take care of this. We will explain to the other candidates that the search is over." The concert was fantastic, and that is how my honeymoon with the Cascade Symphony began.

The most important thing I have learned during my tenure with the Cascade Symphony is how wonderful these people are. In addition to their great human qualities, I am amazed by their dedication

Cascade Symphony Orchestra

to the orchestra. When I first started working with the orchestra, there were a few members who had played in it since the orchestra's inception (and still continue to play!). Many members work full-time all day, and then come to our evening rehearsal, never showing any signs of being tired. From day one it was, and still is, a real blessing for me to work with them.

My life took on a new and exciting direction. I witnessed a miracle happening at the rehearsals, when from the chaotic first reading we slowly moved to the joyful territory of near-perfection. It was incredibly fun to witness how an unorganized mass of sound shaped itself into real music, sometimes within minutes. Again I experienced a feeling of happiness. It was so exciting to be able to create beauty with these wonderful musicians, and I saw in their eyes the same joyful fire. A few years later, conductor Robert Anderson, the founder of the orchestra, came to me after a concert and said something I'll never forget: "Michael, do you understand what you are doing?" My first thought was, "What did I do wrong?"

He took my hand, looked deeply into my eyes, and said slowly, "You are changing people's lives." These words struck me like lightning. Along with a warm wave of contentedness came a feeling of enormous responsibility.

With great enthusiasm I started working on programming, marketing, and all other aspects of the orchestra's life. The audience was coming back. We created a competition for young musicians, calling it the Rising Star Competition, and let the winners play with the orchestra. We recorded the orchestra's first CD, *Symphonic Treasures*, performed at Benaroya Hall, collaborated with ballet and choral companies, hired the best soloists, and published the orchestra's first cookbook, *Measures and Pleasures*. The whole edition is sold out now and has become a rarity.

An especially exciting project came along in the form of a collaboration with Rick Steves, a world-famous travel guru and long-time friend of mine. We have known each other since our kids went to Lakeside School together. We decided to create a project that had never been done before. Rick called it *Europe, a Symphonic Journey*. He provided the visuals and narration, and the orchestra played great musical works from each country in the travelogue.

It was an enormous success. The CD and DVD were recorded,

and the whole program was presented on public television, and broadcast all over the United States. The whole community was surprised and impressed by this unique project.

Here is what Rick Steves had to say about it:

"My mom always told me it's worth dressing up for a special occasion, and this one certainly fit the bill: sharing the stage with a symphony orchestra and its suave conductor, introducing America to Europe's most soul-stirring, heartbeat-quickening, patriotic music. Starting as one of those crazy "sketched on a napkin" ideas, I had the pleasure of collaborating with the Cascade Symphony Orchestra and Music Director Michael Miropolsky. Together we brainstormed, planned, rehearsed, and embarked on a symphonic journey through 19th-century Europe, touching down in seven different countries."

An unexpected miracle followed: Rick Steves decided to make an extremely generous contribution to the Cascade Symphony and the Edmonds Center for the Arts where we performed. It was the largest gift ever made to a community orchestra by an individual. Rick Steves' gift made it possible for the Cascade Symphony to secure its financial future for at least the next two decades.

Our audience continued to grow and the last four seasons were all sold out. We keep receiving a river of overwhelming response from people, and it's very rewarding to hear their excitement about our concerts, especially from people coming from far away and even from out of state.

Here are just a few from the audience:

"Dear Mr. Miropolsky,

...I loved last night's concert. I feel as though you personally are playing to me, and that I can watch how the orchestra created magic."

"...This was a performance in every sense of the word. Cascade does not merely play tunes. Music Director Michael Miropolsky has earned the title "Maestro" giving a well-rounded performance. I know that most conductors have an air of arrogance about them, but Miropolsky is here for the love of music. A love he is happy to share."

"...I found Michael Miropolsky to be extremely entertaining. What a gem. I came expecting to hear good music. I left having heard great music, being thoroughly entertained and with a great respect for the CSO."

"...That is a fabulous, fabulous orchestra!"

"...Marvelous music enhanced by the warmth and personality of the excellent conductor who truly makes the audience feel part of the experience. A community treasure in my backyard. What a discovery!"

And from the musicians:

"Dear Michael,

... You have helped us grow so much in the past years, and have been deeply appreciated and admired, and it's certainly only fair that we "let" you grow and prosper as well! (Kind of hard initially to have to admit that you really don't "belong" to us exclusively!) You are a treasure to all of the CSO, and I hope our joint venture lasts for many more years!"

"...The "word" is out in this community about how delightful you are to play under. I have been telling friends and colleagues for years now about you. From my viewpoint in the back row I thoroughly enjoy sitting, listening, and watching you work with our orchestra. I tell my friends that it is like going to a conducting clinic each week – what you say, how you say it, your consistent tempos, consistent cues, pitch perfect singing and, especially, how your rehearsal schedule and actual rehearsals are so efficient! Sometimes I wonder if you are going to get through everything on the schedule and you always do!"

"...We have grown in so many ways because of who you are. NEVER in our collective 40+ years of being in the CSO have we enjoyed rehearsals and concerts, grown as musicians, or benefitted from the character qualities of our conductor as much as we have during your tenure. We want it "forever!" We respect that you are in demand and

favored by other fortunate ensembles. We will share you with everybody, as it benefits you, but we hope you will ALWAYS be "ours."

With fine performances of the greatest masterpieces we not only provide audiences with education and joy, but build the future of our community. And it is indeed an enormous responsibility!

Playing around at the Cascade Symphony Gala

39 · Family Travels

During the time when Larisa and her family were awaiting permission to leave the Soviet Union, none of them were allowed to travel abroad. This is how I explain the hunger of many Russian immigrants for travel. Larisa was not an exception. She wanted to see the world, and though I traveled a lot during the same years that Larisa's family was in refusenik status, I did not see much on my tours. The orchestra's travel schedule was always intense, typically one concert a day in a different city, and most of my travel memories are associated with concert venues and what we saw from the windows of the tour bus.

We began with Harrison Hot Springs in Canada, and fell in love with the place. Just under three hours' pleasant drive from home, we sometimes visited the area two or even three times a year. The beautiful lake surrounded by mountains gives a feeling of calmness and peace. The air is so pure, and we adored the five pools at the resort. We would spend hours every day soaking in the mineral water. We learned that the best time to be there was in the winter. Sitting in the hot pools with freezing air surrounding you felt amazing. It rained a lot in the winter, too. The moment the ice-cold drops began to fall was most exciting. We would bring a big umbrella, and as the rain hit, we felt like we were in a greenhouse.

Then we took a longer trip to Banff and Jasper, two Canadian national parks, where the animals would come to our cars and eat from our hands. We watched huge brown bears from a distance, but nobody wanted to feed them. As every Seattleite does, we drove to Mount Rainier to experience how monumental it is. Every time we flew from Seattle, it was fascinating to observe the same Mount Rainier from the window of the plane. We looked down on an eternal snow and lunar landscape. The view was almost post-apocalyptic looking. On Highway 101 we drove along the Oregon coast, and I have to admit that I have never in my life seen anything more breathtaking than the view of the ocean from the top of those cliffs.

Our first and (so far) only trip to Hawaii was not so successful. Alex was one year old and the poor little guy got sick on the second

day after we arrived in Maui. In addition to our troubles, on the
third day of our stay the hotel lost power, and we could not even
warm up his baby food. Fortunately the hotel administration was
able to find a room for us in a different hotel and we got to move to
more comfortable accommodations.

We took a trip to Ashkelon, Israel to visit my mother, sister, and
brother-in-law. My dad had passed away, and I wanted my mom
to see her grandkids (that was the only time she would get to see
them). We were already tired after the first long flight to London
with eight hours' jet lag. It was afternoon in London, and nighttime
in Seattle. In order to spend a few hours before the second flight we
took a bus tour of the city. I remember two things: first, both kids
(eight and five years old at the time) got on the bus and instantly
dropped their heads to their chests; secondly, when we were asked
to get off the bus. Turns out we all had a nice ninety-minute nap.

The second flight from London to Tel Aviv also proved long
and exhausting. On the plane I noticed a number of Orthodox
Jews. Just a few minutes after we took off and the captain allowed
the passengers to unbuckle their seat belts, these men jumped out
of their seats and ran to occupy the open seats, obviously a drill that
they performed regularly. They lay down, each occupying three
seats. Soon my kids grew very tired, and I sought mercy from these
men to move a bit and let my kids rest in a more comfortable position. The men totally ignored me, not budging from their seats until the plane landed. It seemed to me that either these men did not
have kids, or they simply didn't feel any sympathy for exhausted
children. As I learned later, on the contrary, all the religious men
had big families and really loved their kids. They just didn't feel
that we were equal to them and deserved any consideration. This
memory still rankles.

We swam in the Dead Sea, with its soapy water that kept everyone afloat. We visited Jerusalem and, as all tourists do, we stuck a
piece of paper with our request to God into a space in the Wailing
Wall. The road from Tel Aviv to the resort city of Eilat was as straight
as an arrow. In the car, I turned the wheel only a few times.

The kids were getting older. When Evelina was in middle school
and Alex was still in elementary, we made a few trips to Europe. It
was a time of paper maps, cars without a navigation system, and

no cell phones. All of our trips were meticulously planned by our friend Leonid Keylin. He had many hobbies, but traveling was by far his favorite. He knew every city, every hotel, every restaurant, and every museum in Europe. He was the internet before the internet. Our itinerary was always crowded and the trips were rather intense; sometimes we crossed the borders of three countries in a day, but we managed to see a lot. On the first trip, I rented a car at the airport. The car had a manual transmission, but in Seattle we were used to cars with automatic transmissions. Before the trip I had an opportunity to drive a stick shift car a couple of times, but it was not enough for me to feel relaxed or in control on the road. The car died every time I tried to get it out of the garage and enter traffic, and the more I tried the more nervous I became. We were suffering from ten hours' jetlag, and my head was not working properly. There was already a line of cars behind me, and they were all honking at me. Finally, as sweaty as a boxer in the ring, I made it.

There was another incident on the same trip. On our way to our hotel, we encountered a serpentine road up a steep hill. I had to change gears the entire way, and at one point the car died, but not completely. When I tried to start and move the car, it started rolling down the hill until we found ourselves on the edge of a cliff. Larisa and the kids were screaming. I put the hand brake on, and asked them to get out of the car. If I die, I thought, at least they will live. Miraculously, I was able to move the car forward, but I still get chills remembering that episode.

Prague impressed us as the most beautiful city in Europe, and the food was superb. But the most delicious goulash we had was in Hungary. In Italy we visited Rome, Florence, Venice, Pisa, Sienna, and many other amazing cities. The abundance of history and beautiful art was overwhelming. Italians were the friendliest people. We could not possibly skip Cremona, the city where 300 years ago the world's most famous violinmakers created instruments that have never been equaled. There are still a lot of violin shops in town (over 100) where contemporary makers try to uncover the mystery of Stradivari and Guarneri. We arrived in Cremona on a Saturday afternoon, planning to stay overnight. I found parking on the plaza (among other cars), and found, to my delight, that parking was free. The hotel was just around the corner, so we took with us only a small bag with necessary things for the night. We had enough time to walk to the central plaza with its huge brick bell tower (the tallest of its kind in the world) and impressive Duomo, a cathedral built many centuries ago. In the morning during breakfast we made our acquaintance with the owner of the hotel, and he asked us where we were heading and if we needed any help with our luggage. I thanked him, and said that the car was around the corner and we had just one bag to carry.

"Where exactly around the corner?" he asked. I did not like his tone. I explained. "No, you cannot park car there. Mercato. Mercato."

"What is mercato?" I asked, growing uneasy.

"Market. Sunday market." I felt a panic rising. Leaving my breakfast unfinished, I ran to the plaza. I turned the corner, expecting to see the same line of parked cars from the night before. As if in a nightmare, yesterday's plaza was completely unrecognizable: it was boiling with hundreds of people. It was the Sunday market. Mercato.

Still refusing to believe what was happening, I went back and forth across the busy plaza, thinking that my car might be parked somewhere, surrounded by shops that had arisen overnight. I came back to the hotel frightened and upset. All of our things for a month of travel were in the car. Fortunately I always carried important documents with me. The hotel owner tried to help me, and explained that the car most likely was towed, but it was Sunday, and Italians don't work on Sunday. After a few telephone calls he still was able to find out where our car was, and gave us a ride to the place. I paid my $100 fine and got the car back with everything inside untouched. So much for free parking!

Driving along the Amalfi Coast was like driving through a dream. Naples confused us when it came to crossing the road. The traffic was going nonstop (remember Caracas?). We came to a crosswalk and started to wait, but there were no stoplights. We waited and waited, and the cars kept going and going. Then some man, obviously a local, just stepped out onto the road and suddenly all the cars stopped as if someone had flipped a switch. We did not dare risk following him, but at some point I just said, "Let's go!" and stepped onto the road. My heart jumped to my throat, but the traffic stopped. How could we have known?

A curious episode occurred in Parma, a central city in the province of Parma, the homeland of famous Parmesan cheese and the last destination of the legendary Italian violinist Niccolò Paganini. It was late afternoon. We had just arrived and were starving, but it was siesta time, which meant that all the stores and restaurants were closed. We had no food in the car and we were tired and cranky, especially the kids. Running from one place to another with the hope of finding some food, we discovered a fancy restaurant, and, already expecting another disappointment, asked if we might get some food.

"Si, signore," we heard. We were so happy! We sat down at the table with a white tablecloth and ordered some pasta. Sometime later the waiter brought us plates of steaming pasta, and we attacked the food. To our surprise the pasta was practically inedible. It was so bad that we called over our waiter. I asked him why the food was so stiff and unpalatable.

"Signore, we don't have a kitchen. We got our food from a nearby place," he answered. We almost choked. How was it possible for any restaurant, especially that nice-looking of a restaurant, to not have its own kitchen? Since then it's become a family joke. If we go out to eat and the food is not good, we say that the restaurant must not have its own kitchen.

Apart from that unfortunate experience, the food in Italy was excellent and very fresh, and one thing was quite a surprise: Italians eat a lot. At lunchtime they would order a big salad, then pizza (one for each person), then a main dish followed by dessert with coffee. Their dinner starts after 8 p.m., and they often eat till midnight. All meals except for breakfast are always accompanied by wine. What's wrong with this picture? Nothing. Watching them eat, I couldn't help but wonder how they never seemed to gain weight! I guess that is the million-dollar question.

In Salzburg, Austria, the city of Mozart, we heard an amazing quartet of Russian balalaika players. They played arrangements of world-famous classical repertoire with passion and sweetness I never imagined possible from a balalaika. Notre Dame de Paris impressed me, but French onion soup did not. We were probably in a touristy place, though there were a lot of French people in that restaurant. In Munich we visited my daughter Yulia. Along with her mother and grandparents, Yulia had immigrated to Germany a few years after I left Russia. Since then, she has become a fine violinist and works with the Munich Symphony Orchestra. She looks just like her mother, with the same olive eyes and smile.

My daughter Yulia

In our travels, everything was supposed to be fun. However, in Nice I was almost killed. Do you want to hear that story? Evelina wanted to try parasailing. Since she was not old enough to do it alone, it was decided that I would go with her. Once we were properly strapped in and outfitted in our gear, we received a brief explanation about how the whole thing worked, and the boat roared as we were lifted in the air.

Because Evelina was far lighter than me, my body went kind of off on one side, and from the first moment I felt very uncomfortable in my seat. I tried to adjust myself, but it did not work. With the pressure of the wind blowing toward us it was not easy. I tried harder and, to my horror, accidentally unbuckled one of the side carabiners. I grabbed the strings of the parachute with a death grip and tried my best not to panic so that Evelina wouldn't know anything was amiss. Screaming for help was not an option: nobody would hear me, and those looking up at me from below would probably mistake my yelling as an expression of excitement. We were probably in the air for no longer than 10 minutes, but it felt like 10 years to me. I felt my grip growing weaker and weaker, and I knew I would fall out of my seat as soon as my hand let go. But many years of practicing violin served me well in strengthening my hands, and I was able to hold on till we landed. Evelina did not notice anything and had a lot of fun, and I made a vow to not come near a parasail again, for as long as I lived.

Costa Rica's lush nature reminded me of the movie *Jurassic Park*. There were monkeys swinging from trees, colorful birds singing everywhere, and real jungles. Only the dinosaurs were missing. Our friend Leonid had recommended we visit a special place. We booked a hotel at the base

Minutes before a near-death experience

of an active volcano. As we swam in the outdoor pool we heard explosions and watched lava and rocks fly through the air. We were told it was safe to be there because the lava came down the other side of the slope, but I still found myself unable to sleep at night and was relieved when we checked out of the hotel several nights later.

The roads in Costa Rica are a special topic. I have never seen such bad roads in my life, not even in Russia. They had ruts and holes sometimes a foot deep. At first I tried to save the car and took pity on my passengers by driving slowly through the holes, but that made our speed close to that of a bicycle. Then I learned that there was another option in which one had to drive through holes and all at full speed. Option "B" worked better, though I almost ruined the car by the end of the second week of our trip.

Monkeys were everywhere. At one place we left our swimsuits to dry outside the bungalow overnight, and they mysteriously disappeared by morning. I guess the monkeys needed some new swim gear.

A long trip to Aruba brought us to an all-inclusive resort. Our room was on ground level, and our door opened up to a magical garden, and a few meters further, a cooling swimming pool. From the beach we could see the coast of Colombia. Humidity was very high; tropical showers arrived so unexpectedly and were so short that we did not have enough time to get out of the pool. The pre-paid all-inclusive nature of our stay made me think of Karl Marx and his utopian idea of communism. All during our stay we forgot that there was any currency in the world. Of course in this version, everything was prepaid by us.

Then there were the cruises. In Mexico, Larisa was stung by a jellyfish. The Alaskan cruise was not great; the food was low qual-ity, and all of the tours were dull and overpriced. One such tour was supposed to take us on the Gold Rush trail. We bought tickets for an old train and for at least an hour had to listen to a lecture about the Gold Rush. The guide pointed a couple of times to a trail along our route, but we could not see anything there but trees and rocks. I guess we were supposed to use our imagination. In addition to the boredom factor, which hit the kids especially hard, the smoke from the coal engine streamed toward us, making us feel sick.

Our cruise to the Caribbean was another brush with death. The ship stopped at the exotic island of Barbados, and we took a boat tour to a smaller island that was covered by volcanic lava. The tour was interesting, but on our way back to the ship a sudden storm hit. Terrible wind, violent rain, and strong waves shook our small boat as we tried to make our way back to the ship. The little boat creaked loudly as I caught the troubled look on the captain's face. Of course we made it, but I bet everybody on the boat was fright-ened to death and praying to a variety of deities.

People go on cruises because for a few days they can see the world while forgetting all about their troubles (and their chores, in-cluding, of course, food preparation and cleaning). Food on cruises is a very special topic. Its unbelievable abundance leads people to eat day and night. Nobody loses weight on a cruise, no matter how hard they try. Each cruise we took had a traditional last-night mid-night buffet that was the pinnacle of a food orgy. After seven days of nonstop eating, a huge crowd collected at the doors of the res-taurant well in advance of midnight. The dining room was deco-rated with four-foot sculptures carved from ice, and on gigantic tables one could find any food imaginable in unending supply.

If you have been on a cruise, then you know what I am talking about; if not – my limited language abilities will not allow me to adequately describe what happened that night. You should experience it yourself. On cruises people can actually lose their health, despite attending the health club onboard. I bet that only a tiny minority of the passengers do any exercise during the trip. (Playing cards while consuming tons of alcohol is not considered exercise.) Nevertheless, I might take a cruise again one day; it's quite an addictive experience, but I know almost for sure that it will be hard for me to resist the sin of gluttony.

40 · Children

We always traveled with our kids. We did this not only because we did not have anyone to leave them with for an extended period of time, but also because we wanted to show them the world. Now they say that they remember some details of our trips, but I am not sure it was worth it. Anyway, we did not have much choice. My memories are full of their constant backseat quarrels, so energizing for them, and so tiring for us parents. Once we went to Canada for two days without them, leaving them at home with a nanny. You know what happened? Ten minutes after we merged onto the freeway, I got a speeding ticket. I was feeling so relaxed, talking without hearing the kids bicker, that I lost track of my speed. That's how we got punished for leaving them behind.

Coming from Russia, I have observed the lives of other musicians who came either from Russia or other countries, and I have come to a simple conclusion: we got our jobs in America only because of our excellent education. Of course, we had talent, millions of hours of practicing, and luck, but without the best training, it is basically impossible for a musician to get a good job here. We decided to give our children the best education we could afford. From the very beginning we put them in private schools. Evelina and Alex had Russian babysitters; we also wanted them to keep the Russian language. When the time came, Alex went to a preschool. He did not know a word of English even though he watched cartoons in English for a good part of the day. He probably understood some of it despite not yet speaking any of the language.

During the first few days when we picked him up after preschool, the teachers told us the same story: that he spoke only Russian with other kids and could not understand why they did not understand him. Soon he picked up English, and later it became a challenge to convince him and Evelina to speak Russian at home. They both attended Russian school on Sundays, and now can speak, read, and write in Russian (probably with the same number of errors I make in English). We signed them up for many activities: karate, piano lessons, Eva – ballet and violin, Alex – cello. Larisa did most of the driving, but always found time to cook dinner and do other chores.

An American mom knows very well what it takes to raise a child, and I admire women's courage and sacrifice. From my observation, I can tell that for the most part, mothers in America are much busier with their kids than fathers. Many women work as much as men do, which makes women in general work more hours a day than men.

We came to this country with a mission: to give our children a better life than we had in Russia. Both Evelina and Alex attended private colleges and I can see that our initial decision about their education was right. I am positive that our hard work to support them will be rewarded. Alex is in his last year of school at Rensselaer Polytechnic Institute and has already received an excellent job offer. Evelina graduated from Whitman College with a degree in psychology and is preparing to pursue her graduate studies at Bastyr University.

With my daughter Evelina backstage at Benaroya Hall

With my son Alex at Lakeside School graduation

41 · BPO, LWSO, TSO

These abbreviations represent the other orchestras I have had the opportunity to conduct. BPO – Bellevue Philharmonic Orchestra – was the only professional orchestra on the Eastside, a fast-growing group of communities across Lake Washington from Seattle. The Eastside, where both Microsoft and Costco are based, is an extremely wealthy area; why could it not sustain a professional orchestra? Due to shortsighted leadership from its board of directors, the orchestra accumulated a deficit beyond its financial reality. Despite strong protest from the musicians, the board declared bankruptcy. Among other things, the orchestra lost its music library, the most valuable asset of any symphony orchestra.

The story of the Bellevue Philharmonic shows how important community support is for arts organizations. I remember we decided to organize a concert at the Bellevue Mall with free admission, so we could attract more potential audience members. The concert went very well, and a decent crowd gathered around the stage. At some point I asked the audience how many of them had ever attended a concert of the Bellevue Philharmonic. Four hands were raised, and I recognized these people; they were four members of the orchestra's board of directors. Let me remind you that the orchestra had been around for more than 40 years, but for some reason it could not find its way into the community's heart.

I received an overwhelming response from the musicians of the Bellevue Philharmonic describing how much they enjoyed working with me, and how upset they were about the orchestra's closure. Here are just a few of them.

"Dear Michael,

When we began working with you I knew you were a fine musician, but I really had no idea what a fine conductor you are as well. I've always felt that you know exactly what you want to hear from the orchestra, which is certainly one of the reasons that your rehearsals are so efficient, and I continue to be impressed with the depth and intelligence of your musical ideas."

"...I have so appreciated working with you the past two years. You are so easy to work with – not easy on us, but very fair and very disciplined in your requirements and your expectations...and I hope our great respect for you was evident."

"...It was an absolute delight working with a conductor who knew the inner workings of an orchestra, who is so enjoyable and inspiring. I have truly appreciated your approach to the orchestra through humor, warmth and professionalism."

"...Your passion for music and positive optimistic approach to the very troubling economic times we find ourselves in inspire me to not give up."

"...I just want to tell you how much I appreciate your excellent conducting, your artistic ideas, your knowledge of string technique and bowing suggestions, but especially your inspiration. It is a pleasure and a joy to play under your baton. I don't know how busy you are, but I hope you can find the time to be our conductor, forever!!"

"...My thanks for a truly enjoyable season at BPO, made possible by you. Your programming, personality, philosophy, professionalism, grace, orchestral playing experience, and respect for the composition, composer, and musicians are so welcome and esteemed by the orchestra. Your willingness and ability to remain positive under changing, less-than-ideal circumstances is remarkable."

"...We all appreciate your excellent musicianship, patience, and sense of humor. Thank you for your hard work, your marvelous musicianship, and for being such a kind, diplomatic person to all of us."

And it was very hard for me to write a goodbye letter to them:

"My Dear Colleagues and Friends,

It is with great sadness that we all learned that the Board of Directors decided to shut down our orchestra. This message is not to analyze why it happened. I am sure that you all know why.

I find it very ironic that we, as an artistic organization, usually only make the headlines twice in our lives: we have a little chance when we are born, and a bigger chance when we die. That is unfortunately the case with the media today. They only cover the "highlights" of our lives. I wish they were more supportive of the arts in our day-by-day struggle for survival.

During our two seasons of music-making, we had the joy to experience an unusually stable and positive relationship between the musicians and the conductor. You know that I am an optimistic person, and I believe that we will have the chance to make more music together in the future. I want to thank you all for a wonderful two years filled with your passionate playing and great patience in order to always achieve the best that we could. I want to thank you for your energy and smiles, for your financial sacrifices and ability to always remain positive and open.

I am currently working on editing the CD we recorded live at our last Pops concert. When I listened to the recorded tracks, I was amazed at how well the orchestra played. It will be a CD of excellent quality and a record of our brilliant achievement. You will be proud of the quality of which our orchestra was capable.

I am happy that I had the honor and privilege to be your friend and your leader during these past two years. I learned a lot from you and am very grateful.

I wish you all the best.

Yours,

Michael"

Two years later, those same musicians, thanks to their hard work, were able to bring the orchestra back, now under a new name: the Lake Washington Symphony Orchestra (LWSO). We have already had two successful and exciting seasons.

In 2013 I also was selected to become the new Music Director of the Thalia Symphony Orchestra (TSO), one of the oldest community orchestras in our area.

42 · Violin versus Baton

In the history of music there are many examples of distinguished musicians trading in their instruments for a conductor's baton. The main reason for this is that these musicians need to express themselves musically beyond what is possible with a solo instrument.

Becoming a conductor requires an early and lengthy musical education. Typically a conductor starts on at least one classical musical instrument (usually as early as age five). Conductors don't start learning actual conducting technique at that early age (though there is quite the display of three-year-old 'genius' conductors on YouTube). To become a conductor, a musician must mature both musically and personally in order to take on the responsibility of leading a large group of well-trained musicians. This requires a thorough mastery of an instrument and the extensive musical education necessary to become proficient in the mysteries of the symphony orchestra.

Some famous conductors, like Leonard Bernstein and Evgeni Svetlanov, began as pianists. Some were string players: Arturo Toscanini was a cellist, Eugene Ormandy a violinist, and Koussevitzky a double bass player. A few conductors even began as singers, most notably Placido Domingo. In rare instances we can find conductors who started out as woodwind, brass, or percussion players.

One significant drawback to a career as a conductor is that in most cases the musicians have to give up their instrument and dedicate themselves entirely to the baton. Rarely do conductors continue to play their musical instruments in the public arena, but some do. The best examples here are the pianist Daniel Barenboim and the late cellist Mstislav Rostropovich, both superb instrumentalists who were also successful behind the podium. But the really great conductors do not return to their instruments to continue a solo career.

My musical career unfolded in a rather unusual way. I developed an interest in conducting during my college years when I had already been playing violin for over 10 years, but did not have the opportunity to pursue conducting as a career. I was allowed to declare only one major (and there was no such thing as a minor) at the Gnessin College, and I did not want to abandon my violin. My real opportunity to conduct, to pursue the long-awaited dream, became possible only when I came to America, but I continued to play the violin and have carried on both careers simultaneously.

As a conductor who also plays almost daily in the region's largest symphony orchestra, I have a special angle from which to observe and analyze the specifics of conducting from the "inside." Sitting on the first stand in the Seattle Symphony Orchestra has allowed me to closely watch and notice every small detail in each conductor's technique, including the several international conductors who arrive each season to guest conduct. I learned the "how to's" and the "how not to's" very quickly. My 25-year history with the Seattle Symphony was probably the best conducting school I ever attended.

Being an orchestra violinist has been a marvelous learning experience, and has given me the invaluable knowledge of how to deal with the orchestra as a conductor. Every word and every gesture I make, I run through the filter of an orchestra musician's ears and eyes. Thanks to my extensive experience as an orchestra musician, I am always able to know what the musicians need from me: what words and what gestures will work best, what tone of voice to use, which passages require the most focus. I also know what I should never say, how I should never conduct or behave, even when occasionally faced with overwhelming temptation to do so.

From the start of my conducting career, I adopted a method of working with the orchestra based on complete respect for the musicians' needs. After rehearsing a certain part, especially one that includes tempo or beat pattern changes (often a most challenging aspect for the conductor from a technical point of view), I always ask the orchestra: is what I'm doing absolutely clear? I insist on them totally understanding my artistic and technical intentions. I believe that every musician in the orchestra has the right to be comfortable with the conductor's ideas. Sometimes one or two musicians express their desire to repeat certain passages and in most cases this means to me that I was not clear enough. It is a good opportunity for me to master my technique by repeating the excerpt while trying a slightly different approach in hopes of making my gestures more clear.

Other rules of conducting I live by include talking as little as possible and instead using my hands in a manner that renders words unnecessary. Only when the hands do not properly communicate my intentions will I use my words. The goal is to encourage, not enforce. If I need to repeat a passage, I always give an explanation as to why I've chosen to do so. Even if it's because the orchestra (or soloist) did not play well, I would never say so, nor would I ever stare at or single out a musician in any way. Instead, I simply say, "Let's try again." Musicians themselves know better than a conductor when they have not performed well. On the other hand, I would never say something was good when I know the orchestra or musician could do better if they tapped into their potential. Additionally, it is important to know the limitations of each musician (as well as the group as a whole) and not to push in a way that exposes these limitations during a performance.

Throughout my years of conducting, only once did I have a curious episode. It happened during a rehearsal with the Cascade Symphony Orchestra. We were working on *Scheherazade* by Rimsky-Korsakov, a very challenging composition not only for the orchestra but for the conductor as well. The instrumentation of the piece calls upon a large orchestra and big percussion section. At some point while rehearsing a difficult passage, I stopped and heard one of the percussion players ask me a question. The question came from an experienced musician who had played in the orchestra for many years.

"Michael, I don't understand what you're doing there." I presume he meant that my gestures were not clear to him. Both the way in which he phrased the question and the tone of his voice were a rather improper way of talking to a conductor. I have a high tolerance when it comes to working with an orchestra (which has been often noted by many musicians with whom I work), and I did not react to the manner in which his question was asked, though I noticed that the other musicians had. Quite a few faces turned toward him in astonishment, and only then did I realize that his way of addressing me was unacceptable, even from the musicians' point of view. The room was thick with tension.

"Which particular bars do you mean?" I asked. This was one of those challenging spots for the conductor, but I thought that I had done alright.

He gave me the bar numbers and I said, "Let's play it again, and I will try to be more clear." We played it again, it sounded good, and I asked that musician if it was any better or clearer this time around. He was satisfied. This could have been the end of a minor episode in the orchestral life, but it was not. I soon forgot about the incident but interestingly enough, the other musicians did not.

The next day I received an email from one of the principal players who also represented the Board of Directors, saying how appalled they were at the inappropriate behavior of that musician. They found his way of approaching the conductor deeply offensive and thought that the musician should be dismissed on the spot. The fact that the musicians were defending the conductor from their colleague came to me as a complete surprise, as it tends to happen the other way around. They were asking for my permission to fire him. I disagreed with their decision and asked the board to honor my request. They acquiesced, but insisted on at least giving him a written warning.

This experience taught me two valuable lessons: if anything goes wrong during a rehearsal or performance, it's the conductor's fault. Secondly, it is important to never lose your temper; finding a kind and rational way to resolve conflict before it becomes a bigger problem is always a better option.

*   *   *

I am grateful that my life turned out this way, allowing me to stay on both sides of the "fence," adding great variety and depth to my musical endeavors.

- **To Baton or not to Baton? (or: From Cane to Toothpick)**

Conducting can be a very dangerous profession. One of the first professional conductors, the 17th-century French composer Jean-Baptiste Lully, became a victim of his passionate conducting style. In Lully's day, the conductors actually led the orchestra facing the audience instead of the orchestra, and they used a five-foot-long conducting staff to thump the rhythm on the floor. Lully accidently struck and pierced his foot with the staff, creating a wound that later caused his death from gangrene. After this terrible incident, conductors decided to protect themselves by inventing the baton, which at first was quite thick but served the additional purpose of whacking musicians on the head when the conductor got angry. Obviously the musicians did not appreciate this in the least bit. Because of their protests and, more likely because it was tiring for the conductor to wave a heavy stick throughout a long symphony, conductors slowly graduated to the much lighter and more elegant version of the baton that we see today.

History knows a number of cases of conductors stabbing themselves, mostly in their hands. After Lully, who might be considered the most infamous conductor in this matter, the list of unfortunates includes Rafael Kubelik, Sir Georg Solti, Jose Serebrier, and Guido Cantelli among others. One time while rehearsing an intensely dramatic Dies Irae in Verdi's *Requiem*, I got so overexcited from the magnificent music and hearing a chorus of 120 people singing in unison that I hit the stand with my right hand. I didn't really pay it any attention, and continued to conduct until the musicians pointed out that my hand was bleeding profusely. I covered the wound with several Band-Aids, and continued the rehearsal.

Yet another danger present is that the conductor might fall off the podium, whether due to overexcitement or inattention (or even drunkenness). This has indeed happened a few times, and many conductors today use a podium with a railing around its perimeter to avoid this hazard. With these adjustments, the conductor's profession remains the safest among all musical professions.

Some conductors work without a baton altogether. A few wonderful conductors, including Dimitri Mitropoulos and Leopold Stokowski, enjoyed brilliant careers without ever having touched a baton. Not only is this the safest way to conduct, but it's also the cheapest. Batons tend to break easily if hit against a music stand. I've broken a few myself.

Some conductors have gone baton-free while still keeping

something in their hand: the famous Russian conductor Valeri Gergiev sometimes conducts with a toothpick! Though he is quite serious about his invention, we have yet to see any followers adopt his approach. I wonder if he uses the same toothpick more than once, or whether he throws the "used" one away after each concert. Maybe he saves them for his fans?

Some conductors go back and forth between using the baton and their hands during a single piece. Some cannot decide for years what works better for them, alternating between the two. Once I saw a conductor leading the orchestra with the baton in his left hand. This was an absolute disaster for the musicians: all the gestures they were used to seeing appeared backwards, a confusing mirror image.

The audience tends to get suspicious when the conductor does not have a baton, and it's understandable: without a baton it looks as if something is missing from the conductor. This is because the baton has become the symbol of the conductor's profession.

I think that conducting without the stick is easier than with it. For me it's almost like playing my violin without a bow, just plucking the strings. This works well for certain pieces, but it has its obvious limitations. It is the bow that holds the complexity of options from which the player is able to draw. It is the bow that makes all the difference in tone color, character, and mood. And it is the baton that shows the level of professional skill the conductor is able to demonstrate. It adds elegance and poetry to the gesture. It helps musicians recognize the conductor's ideas and intentions. It elevates the image of the person on the podium. And finally it gives the audience more pleasure to watch that strange person in front of the orchestra, the only one without a musical instrument in his hands, but whose magic stick is able to unify all instruments and reveal the thrilling mystery hidden in the score.

• To Sweat or Not to Sweat?

Some conductors have become famous for using such small gestures on the podium that it's difficult for the musicians to see them, not to mention the audience. One such conductor was Fritz Reiner, who in the 1950s and 1960s held the post of Music Director of one of the finest American symphony orchestras, the Chicago Symphony. His gestures were so tiny that he might be considered the champion of minimalist conducting. The following story is true, and it is both funny and sad.

A new cellist was hired to play with the Chicago Symphony and was placed on the last stand of the cello section. At his first rehearsal he could not see Reiner's gestures at all, but he did his best to play along with the section and not stick out. This cellist was not without imagination, but also had a chip on his shoulder. On the next day he brought to rehearsal a pair of large binoculars and, at some point, started using them to watch the conductor. This undoubtedly helped him to identify Reiner's beat; however, it did not go unnoticed by the conductor. Still, Reiner did not display even the smallest reaction to the musician's behavior. On the next day, the same cellist pulled out his binoculars again. Without stopping his conducting, Rainer silently pulled from his pocket a piece of paper and turned it toward the cellist. On the paper was written, "You're fired!"

On the other hand there are conductors who love to grimace and make wild gesticulations, to the point that the musicians are distracted. However, this sort of behavior does tend to greatly impress the audience. Musicians know that these conductors conduct neither for them nor for the music, but for the audience. Needless to mention, the musicians are not impressed. These types of conductors tend to sweat a lot, but the orchestra remains cold. A well-known Russian conductor had his own opinion on this sort of conducting. His favorite expression was, "When I conduct I don't sweat, but the orchestra should!"

There should be a fine balance between conductor's body motions, facial expressions, and verbal explanation of his intentions. Not too many have the gift to achieve such a fine balance.

• Orchestra Player versus Conductor

The most basic responsibility of the orchestra players is practicing their part until it is note-perfect. Players are not required to demonstrate any additional knowledge about the piece, composer, history, or style (though they certainly may do so). Orchestra musicians have to listen to their playing, listen to what is going around them, and follow their instincts, but most of all – they must watch the conductor.

The musician's job is introverted by nature. An orchestra musician cannot entirely know what they contribute on an individual level. You simply cannot hear yourself well enough in the orchestra. Expressing your individuality is not allowed, of course, because the most valuable quality is the ability to follow the conductor's concept of the music and to blend into a big, collective sound. As a result, the job is not creative on a certain level, and this frustrates players who have always considered music making to be a creative process. (On the other hand, any conductor-free performance in a smaller group, such as a chamber ensemble, instantly sparks a creative process. As soon as there is a conductor in front of the musicians, the whole concept of creation is taken away from the musicians and passed into the hands of the conductor.)

There are some perks of being an orchestra player as opposed to a conductor. The greatest is the feeling of the physical touch of the instrument. The musician makes the instrument come to life, feels its living vibrations, and forms the shape, color, and volume of the sound. It is a very intimate and rewarding feeling. That is why musicians are always trying to find better quality instruments, and also to find an instrument that fits them like a glove and becomes a beloved partner in music. This kind of musical intimacy is foreign to the conductor.

The conductor's world, his mentality and his job, are in opposition to that of the orchestral musician's. A conductor not only has to learn a score to the last detail in all its complexity, but also the history of the piece and its composer, the style of the period, and its great performances of the past. This requires collecting a lot of information. The conductor's artistic images are born inside of him, and have to be projected onto the players. His will should radiate all the time from within, and the stronger this projection, the more powerfully received this message will be by the musicians. He is at all times a creator, whether studying the score at home or performing the piece at a concert. A conductor has no days off. Music is always in his head; the creative process never ceases. All of this makes his job extremely complex and saddles him with great responsibility, but is in the end extremely satisfying. The greatest challenge of this most controversial musical profession has been and always will be the ability to inspire the musicians. This requires a great deal of talent.

43 · Seattle: The Northwest City

One of the things I fear the most caught me in Seattle: an earthquake. February, 2001. I was on the phone with my friend, and suddenly heard him yell, "Earthquake!" before the connection was lost. I was alone at home, and ran out of the house to the backyard. The earth's movement was so strong that I could not keep my balance and had to sit down on the ground. Our house was moving in front of my eyes, and the beating of my heart had never been louder. When the shaking stopped, I reentered the house. The chandelier was still waltzing from left to right, but nothing appeared broken. Our house sits close to the very top of Magnolia Hill, and I had a good view of nearby Queen Anne Hill from the window. The view was both amazing and terrifying: the whole of Queen Anne Hill was moving like an ocean in a storm. Big waves were rolling across the hill, something I had never seen in my life, not even in my nightmares. Gradually the waves diminished, and everything returned to normal, except for a fear that has never left my mind since.

At the moment the earthquake struck, Larisa had an orthodontist appointment, and was caught lying in the orthodontist's chair with her mouth open. The doctor was in the middle of making an impression of Larisa's teeth. He had put the soft modeling material into her mouth, and told Larisa to wait a few minutes in stillness that so the mold could set. When the office staff felt the quake, they all ran out of the building and left Larisa lying in the chair. That was both a comical and an unsettling situation; a patient lying with her mouth open, unable to move. It took us forever to pick the kids up from their schools; the traffic was unbelievable, almost the "normal" heavy traffic of today.

When we came to Seattle, our new friends introduced us to one of their favorite places: Costco. Many years later this store still surprises me. At Costco I have run into not only my colleagues, and neighbors, but on a couple of occasions I even met Jack and Becky Benaroya, very wealthy people and among Seattle's most generous philanthropists. (They gave more than $15 million to launch the construction of the Seattle Symphony's concert hall, Benaroya Hall.) In one way, shopping at Costco reminded me of shopping in

Russia. In Russia, if you want to buy a sausage, you go to the grocery store and there is no sausage there, but across the street you see a big line of people, and you join this line, and you end up buying a pair of winter boots. It's not exactly the same in Costco, but when you go there to buy some balsamic vinegar or olive oil, you end up with a full shopping cart at the register, shelling out $250.

In Seattle I started to learn about the stock market. This experience, like many others, was absolutely unavailable to me back in Russia. I got very excited when the market was rising a hundred points every day, and the entire world joined me in that crazy rally. Then, when the market plunged, I learned another lesson, and the whole world joined me again, and a few years' worth of our savings evaporated into thin air. Larisa was not happy. Neither was I, but I learned that we always pay for our lessons, and unfortunately, that lesson was an especially expensive one.

Once upon a time we had cable television. Evelina was four years old and Alex still a baby, and Halloween was coming up. All the channels were running scary movies about that strange holiday. I had some free time and joined my children in watching one of those movies. It so happened that the story was about some children who were abducted by vampires. I grew so emotional feeling my defenseless children next to me, and imagined them disappearing. I turned the TV off, and since then I cannot stand this holiday. The power of art!

44 · Cloudy

I bet that almost every American family has or has had, at some point, a pet. We went through this experience as well. When the time came, my kids started begging me for a cat. Coincidently, a friend of ours had found a kitten on the street, and gave it to us. It was an adorable puffy ball of fur with tiny but very sharp claws. To rid the kitten of possible fleas, I gave her a bath. She hated it, and scratched me without mercy. At the end of the bathing session the shower curtain looked like it had gone through a shredder.

The kitten looked like a grey cloud with beautiful long fur, and the name for her quickly came to mind: Cloudy. She became an indoor cat, and we had the choice to declaw her or trim her nails ourselves. I chose the latter. Cloudy was never fond of that procedure, but she knew that it was inevitable, and lying on her back, from time to time she just hissed at me to show her disapproval.

We found a Russian alternative name for Cloudy, Klava, and she graciously responded to it, especially when I was headed to the fridge to get her favorite food, canned fish. With her tail standing straight as an arrow she would meow so loudly that our neighbors knew – it's dinnertime!

She had an amazing personality, a combination of independence like all cats have, fear of any new person in the house, and endless tenderness. When it was time to cut her nails or clean up after her, Cloudy was daddy's cat. When it was time for cuddling, playing, and kissing, she was Evelina's cat.

When I would come home from work, Cloudy would already be sitting on the stairs across from the main entrance, extending her little head forward with curious eyes, almost asking, "What kinds of tasty smells from the outside world did you bring today?" She would sniff my head and hands, and not finding anything delicious, jump like a bullet back to her safe place in Evelina's bed.

Cloudy did not like our music at home; it was probably too loud for her sensitive cat ears. A couple of times she managed to escape from the house, but always returned home with a dirty coat of fur full of leaves. Just one time we could not find her. She had climbed up a tree, probably running away from a dog, and I had to rescue her with a ladder.

Sometime after what we thought was Cloudy's 15th birthday (we did not know exactly when she was born), we noticed a change in her behavior. She became slower in her movements and her meows sounded sad. She started to eat less, and soon stopped drinking water. She was melting away day by day. Cloudy had a long and happy cat's life. When she died, I cried, cried, cried...

45 · *Auer, Reuven and Jascha*

I am holding in my hands a unique document. It is Leopold Auer's business card. On it is printed: "L. S. Auer – Soloist of His Emperor's Majesty" with the address in the lower right corner, "26, English Prospect." Handwritten in Russian, it declares, "I am accepting to my class without fee Reuven and Jascha Heifetz," with Auer's signature and a date, "3/1914." The year was corrected by hand to, "1915" (or the other way around, it's hard to say). The card has a thick layer of glue on the back because it was extracted from the family album, where it had been sitting for almost 80 years. The paper has become slightly yellowish; otherwise it's in perfect condition.

Leopold Auer's business card

How did this rare document end up in my hands?

Just a couple of months before we were going to leave Russia, Larisa had a meeting with a woman who was also preparing for emigration. This woman told Larisa that she was a distant relative of Jascha Heifetz. She had a large collection of documents related to the world's most famous violinist, but she did not think of them as anything of value, and now that she was going through her papers, she was simply throwing them away. It seemed that she was not totally in her right mind; this was perhaps the only reason that would explain her putting all that Heifetz memorabilia into the trash. Larisa humbly asked permission to rescue the papers and the woman gave all of them to her without any regret. That's how these unique documents came into our family. Among the fascinating collection, this business card stands out as the most intriguing document, and supports the story of how a teenage Jascha got into the class of the most important Russian violin teacher of the time at the St. Petersburg Conservatory.

The story goes like this: Jascha started playing violin very young, when he was three. By the age of nine, he was already a child prodigy. At the age of 11 he made his debut with the Berlin Philharmonic under the direction of the great conductor, Arthur Nikisch, performing the Tchaikovsky Violin Concerto. But his father, Reuven, clearly understood that Jascha was still a child who needed strong artistic guidance. His future mentor would become Professor Leopold Auer, whose class of 30 students included the best violinists of the 20th century: Mischa Elman, Efrem Zimbalist, Nathan Milstein, Toscha Seidel, and Miron Poliakin, among others.

In the Czar's Russia, Jews were only allowed to live in certain territories. Moscow and St. Petersburg were off-limits unless they had legitimate official business or were admitted to the colleges. Jascha, who was Jewish like the violinists listed above, was admitted to the conservatory based on his extraordinary talent and reputation as a child prodigy. But he was too young to live in the city alone, and according to the law could not be separated from his family.

Like a grandmaster in a chess game, Auer made a brilliant move: he accepted Reuven, Jascha's father (who was also a violinist) into his class. This way, the Heifetz family would be allowed to live in St. Petersburg, and that would allow Auer to teach young Jascha as well. That explains the message on the business card. It's not clear whether Reuven ever appeared in Auer's class with his fiddle (probably not), but he brought his son to lessons with the professor, and patiently waited at the door until the class was over. It could be one hour or it could be three; Auer took Jascha very seriously. Just a few years later, the young virtuoso would become a champion among all the violinists of the 20th century.

Right after the Great October Socialist Revolution in 1917 when the Bolsheviks overthrew the Czar and started building their "fair and equal" society, Leopold Auer, who was not only a great teacher and wonderful violinist himself, but also a man with a big vision, would take all of his class with him and immigrate to America. He had foreseen the potential outcome out of the communist social experiment.

Historians affirm that Jascha never practiced exercises or any technical work while studying with Auer. He built his phenomenal technique playing pieces and concertos alone. In this light, Jascha's own statement sounds even more curious. Once he was asked what he would play if he had only one hour to practice before a concert. His answer was, "Fifty minutes of scales and ten minutes on the rest of the program."

Jascha Heifetz would be recognized as the "King of the Violin" and become the highest paid musician of his time, playing an average of 200 concerts a year.

Holding this business card makes my hands tremble. The card carries the DNA of the people who are legends in the history of music. The idea that my DNA is now mixing with theirs gives me a feeling similar to what I experience before going on stage: anxiety and excitement.

46 · Jean-Baptiste Vuillaume

During my tenure with the Seattle Symphony Orchestra I have had the privilege of meeting some extraordinary people who recognize the value of classical music and generously support the arts in our community. On many occasions I have had enjoyable conversations with Jack and Becky Benaroya, Sam and Althea Stroum, Sam and Gladys Rubinstein, Craig and Joan Watjen (who financed the construction of the magnificent concert organ at Benaroya Hall), Microsoft founder Bill Gates, billionaire software genius Charles Simonyi, and many others. It was wonderful to see how much passion these remarkable people had for music and the Seattle Symphony. Some of them also became sponsors of the groups that I led: the Seattle Violin Virtuosi and the Cascade Symphony Orchestra.

I was very excited when I learned about the opportunity to play unique violins from the collection of David Fulton, a wonderful violinist and a generous Seattle Symphony supporter. It was hard to believe that I had in my hands instruments made by the unsurpassable Stradivari and Guarneri, instruments that once belonged to the legendary virtuosos Fritz Kreisler, Isaac Stern, Yehudi Menuhin, and Itzhak Perlman. It was a thrilling experience. I felt that the violins themselves were telling me how to play them, as if they possessed a will of their own. Holding them was a tremendously powerful emotional experience. These instruments are now worth millions and millions of dollars, but in reality, they are priceless.

For a long time I searched for a violin for myself that a) I really liked, and b) could afford. The second point really brought me back down to earth. Every string player knows that such a search has the potential to become a lifelong adventure. Finding an instrument with which to fall in love is like finding a true friend, one that will last you a lifetime. (By this time we had found Larisa a very fine early 20th century violin – this time not a fake! – by Italian Alfredo Contino.)

The first violin I bought in Seattle was made by a very good Russian-American maker, Boris Sverdlik. It was beautiful and had amazing articulation. The notes under my fingers bounced off the fingerboard. The violin had a clear and happy soprano tone, but I soon realized that my ear was hungry for a darker tone. My next violin was created by French maker Georges Chanot. It had a darker tone and for a couple of years I liked its sound, but it was still missing that balance between clear articulation, depth, and warmth of tone and at that point I was simply looking for a better quality instrument.

One day I got a call from a violin dealer. I received such calls from time to time from different violin shops since people knew I was in the market for a good violin. I asked what she had to offer, and she said that she had a fine violin by French maker Jean-Baptiste Vuillaume. Having tried a few of them in the past, I knew they were within my price range but I didn't like their big and hollow sound. "I am not interested," I told her, but she said that she was passing through the city and my house was on her way. I thought it would be impolite to turn her down.

Jean-Baptiste Vuillaume was one of the finest violinmakers and brilliant music innovators in musical history. He is considered to be second only to the "French Stradivarius," Nicolas Lupot. History books say that during his lifetime Vuillaume made 3,000 violins, forever searching for the secrets of the great Italians. Like any violinmaker he was totally obsessed with the idea of finding these out, but Stradivari and Guarneri took their secrets to the grave. As part of his research, Vuillaume would buy the finest Italian violins and perform "surgery" on them, melting the varnish, taking off the so-called ground, and unfortunately often destroying these instruments in the process. He was a rich violinmaker and could afford to buy the best and most expensive instruments for his experiments. Who knows how many of the finest instruments were destroyed by him?

Legend has it that Niccolò Paganini once brought Vuillaume his beautiful Guarneri to be fixed, but upon receiving his instrument a few days later and playing it Paganini realized that it was not his violin but a perfect copy of his Guarneri! Vuillaume was so good at his craft that he was able to make an exact replica of the Italian virtuoso's violin down to its sound, and play this playful prank on his client. As interesting as this tale is, it's hard to believe that a violin player (especially Paganini) would be fooled even by the greatest luthier of the time to the point that he would not have recognized his own violin. Paganini later gifted this replica to his only student, Camillo Sivori.[7]

When the woman opened up the case, I instantly liked the look of the instrument. It had an elegant shape with a one-piece back, beautiful sliding lines on the wood, light brown varnish, and a noble golden reflection. Its arching was amazingly flat which usually increases the instrument's ability to project its sound. The violin was made in 1845 and bore the signature of Vuillaume. For a 155-year-old violin it was in amazing condition, and as I later learned it had been created based on the pattern of the famous Giuseppe Guarneri's violin called "Cannon" (the same violin Paganini had given Vuillaume for repair!)

I took the violin into my hands and drew the bow across its open strings. The violin answered me with a strong resonance. Then I started to play Massenet's *Meditation* from his opera *Thais*, which is a good test for any violin.[8]

I loved the sound of the instrument: it was bright enough on the E string, rich and dark on the G string, had the perfect color and volume balance. It was deep and passionate, not what I expected from Vuillaume. I got an incredible feeling that the violin was speaking to me, and I knew this was it. Today, fifteen years later, my initial impression remains the same: both the look and sound of the instrument appeal greatly to me. I had found a great friend, one that will last me a lifetime. It was love at first sight. I count myself incredibly lucky.

---

7 These days even top violin experts are sometimes mistaken when identifying great Italian instruments. There is the possibility that some of the old Cremona instruments are not authentic, but actually copies made by Vuillaume.

8 This five-minute piece of tremendous tenderness and beauty "escaped" from the opera and took on a life of its own. It made Massenet's name widely known, especially among violinists, since in the opera the solo violin performs this melody.

47 · *Sticks with Horsehair*

In my college years in Moscow I was told that if I couldn't afford a good violin then I should at least invest my money in a proper bow. I even don't remember what kind of bow I had at that time, probably a cheap one made in a Czech factory that music stores sold for just three rubles apiece (to re-hair a bow cost five rubles!). One day, my orchestra colleague and friend Kostya Stolyarevsky, who was aware of my bow situation, gifted me his bow: a gem crafted by the well-known German bow maker Ludwig Bausch. It was far superior to mine, heavier and much stronger. I loved that bow. I cherished this gift dearly. Later, when I came to America, I learned that this bow had a crack, was heavily worn out near the frog, had poor balance and was twisted. Its condition was such that it had almost no monetary value.

As time went on, I tried out many other bows. I learned that in order for it to qualify as a good bow, it has to not only fit and feel comfortable in the musician's hand, but also fit the violin itself. Violins are generally divided into two categories: those with a darker tone, and those with a brighter, soprano tone. The bow must balance the sound of the violin. If the violin has a darker sound, the bow should make it sound brighter, and the other way around. Other considerations include a balance that allows strokes to come more easily, a good grip, and the ability to draw a nice tone. It also helps for it to be in good condition, which would increase its resale value, and to have no history of repairs. A bow that has been cracked or broken (especially at the tip) loses almost 90% of its value.

I was lucky. Since the accident at my music school in Frunze when I forgot to lock the case and my violin fell out of it, it hadn't happened again. The bow did slip out of my hands a few times, fortunately landing on the floor without damage. A couple of times I managed to react so quickly that I caught the bow in midair.

Why do some violinists carry up to four bows in their case? Each bow has slightly different weight and character. Depending on the music being performed, the musician will choose the bow that best fits the piece. A lighter bow serves well for a classical piece like a symphony by Haydn or Mozart; a stronger and heavier bow will draw more tone and better suit a romantic or modern piece.

Rehairing the bow is a story of its own. Since the hair wears out when the bow is drawn against the string, every couple of months (assuming that the player practices two to three hours a day) the bow starts to lose its grip. The rosin does not hold on the bow anymore and the bow will start to literally slide along the string. Performing short, bouncing strokes like spiccato becomes increasingly difficult, clarity is lost, and the tone of the instrument becomes more shallow.

The process of rehairing requires a highly skilled professional. After finding the finest horsehair, one must select and brush approximately 120 pieces of it before installing it into the bow. Experienced string players can always tell whether a bow was rehaired by a skillful master and if it has good quality hair.

When I came to Seattle in 1991 I discovered that the Rainy City was famous not only for Microsoft, Boeing, Starbucks and the Seattle Opera's productions of Wagner's *Ring*, but also as a center of rising bow makers. A group of talented masters had made their home in nearby Port Townsend. Soon I acquired a very good bow from one of them, Charles Espey, and began to practice with it. After some time I began to feel that the bow was not quite flexible enough for me, and I began to look for another bow. That is how I met an exceptionally talented bow maker, a young fellow by the name of Keith Peck.

Keith was shy and very friendly and adored his job. He worked in two directions. As all young bow makers attempted to do, Keith established his own style by creating a new bow pattern. He experimented with types of wood, the bow's balance, and shapes of the frog. He even made a few bows using amber for the frog. These bows were extremely beautiful. His greatest success, however, was in imitating bows of the great French makers, especially those of Dominique Peccatte. I was very excited by the idea of owning such a bow and asked Keith to make me two: one for myself and one for Larisa. To our luck, the first bow was ready in a week, but we waited a few more months for the second one to be completed.

Both bows were the epitome of fine craftsmanship, each with its own unique character. They had excellent balance and tone quality. These bows became our favorites, and with their amazing combination of flexibility and strength, as well as the ability to draw a beautiful tone from the violin, I consider them the best Keith Peck ever made. Two decades later they still have a place in my violin case along with a couple of French bows that I bought at a later time.

Unfortunately Keith Peck's life was short. He died suddenly in his shop at the age of forty-five while working on a new bow. His untimely death was a shock to the musicians who knew him. We lost a wonderful friend and phenomenally gifted master of bow making.

I later had the privilege of playing with authentic bows created by the legendary Dominique Peccatte and Francois Tourte from the collection of David Fulton. The experience was overwhelming. Paired with the best violins one could imagine (Fulton had a few violins by Stradivari and Guarneri del Jesú), the sound these bows made can only be described as butter, honey, and chocolate. I was especially impressed with the bow by Francois Tourte. The most famous bow maker of all time, Francois Tourte has been called the "Stradivari of the Bow." His remarkable bows are very rare, hitting close to the $300,000 mark at music auctions. To appreciate the quality of these finest bows, the player must embark on a long journey of learning about the history of bow making before having the opportunity to play with them. Only after many years of such experience can one fully understand the uniqueness of these masterpieces: sticks with horsehair.

48 · The John and Carmen Delo
Assistant Principal Second Violin

When musicians come onstage to play a concert, the first thing they do is look out into the hall. Is it going to be full? Is the audience already excited about the program? Did they come to hear the famous soloist or us, the orchestra? We are like a thermometer checking the emotional temperature in the hall. Sometimes we will find a familiar face in the audience and send a smile. Every concert is different, but we know pretty much how it will go even before the concertmaster comes on stage and the first oboist gives the "A." After some time we learn where the most devoted people sit, since they come to almost every concert, and usually keep the same seats from season to season, almost like those of us in the orchestra.

It was the beginning of the 2003-04 season when I noticed an interesting couple. They always sat in the same place in one of the front rows, and we had a good view of each other. They always watched me enter the stage, and somehow I got the feeling that they were waiting for me. The man appeared especially excited when he saw me; he would start waving at me, and I would smile in response. This became almost a ritual: I come on stage, the man waves at me, I smile.

One time at the beginning of intermission, Seattle Symphony Executive Director Deborah Card approached me and in a very excited voice told me that she wanted to introduce me to some people.

"Now?" I asked.

"Yes, yes, now, please!"

"What is happening?"

"These people just announced that they want to endow your chair!"

This was quite a shock to me. I had never expected that my chair would be endowed. In simple terms, it means that an individual or a corporation really liked a particular player, and agreed to donate a lot of money to the endowment fund of the orchestra, so that their name would be printed in the orchestra roster next to the name of their favorite musician. In the past, it had always been a principal player, and I was not a principal. In our second violin section the principal chair was not yet endowed. I asked Deborah, "Why me, why not the principal?" She said, "I asked them about endowing the principal chair, but they absolutely refused. They said they will give money on your behalf or not at all."

"I guess we'd better meet these people," I responded.

To my huge surprise, when we entered the Green Room, I saw the same couple who had been waving to me all the time. They were introduced to me as John and Carmen Delo. I told them how excited and grateful I was for their generous contribution. It seemed that they were even more excited and happy to meet me for the first time, since we had never said a word to each other before.

The intermission was coming to an end, and I had to hurry to get back to my seat. On the way back I asked Deborah again, "Why me?" She responded, "They said that they liked your smile." At that moment I fully realized the meaning of the American expression, "A million-dollar smile."

Later I got to know the Delos better and we became good friends. I learned how passionate and excited they were about classical music. They were both retired and literally filled their lives with music. Each day they attended concerts, ballets, or operas. When Carmen passed away I played *Meditation* from *Thais* for her memorial ceremony. I wish I could do more to honor the memory of that truly devoted music lover and friend.

With John and Carmen Delo, who endowed my chair at the
Seattle Symphony Orchestra

49 · Tragedy

When we look at other people or their families we rarely notice, or perhaps we cannot see, what is really going on in their lives.
Mostly we see what is on the surface, and on the surface it's "fine."
People tend not to expose what is negative in their lives. But I believe that in the life of each person and in each family there are
bad and often tragic things that have happened, and these people
carry that heavy baggage with unhealable wounds through the rest
of their lives.

A tragedy also occurred in our family. When the doctor diagnosed Larisa with stomach cancer, he said that for such a type and
size of tumor, it takes years or even decades to develop. Larisa never
missed an annual checkup, and her most recent tests had been fine.
She had a history of stomach ulcers starting when she was twenty,
and they bothered her from time to time. Extra stress (and there
was plenty of it in her life) aggravated the pain in her stomach.
Mylanta eased the pain and Larisa continued to rally. The only reason we decided to schedule a doctor's appointment was because
every time Larisa ate, she would get bad heartburn. There were absolutely no other symptoms.

We started to fight the cancer. An operation was not possible
since the tumor took up almost the whole stomach, and a round
of chemotherapy was scheduled. This made the tumor shrink and
then surgery was performed. Almost her entire stomach was removed, and then Larisa had a second round of chemotherapy. The
side effects of the treatment were terrible, and when the doctor said
that the cancer had spread and suggested another round of chemo,
Larisa refused. It was clear that we had lost the battle.

During those exhausting six months of her fight, I saw an amazing transformation in Larisa's character. She grew calmer, more
patient, more forgiving, and never, ever stopped caring for our
children and me. This transformation happened thanks to a very
special person, Lada Schuiski, who opened my and Larisa's eyes to
a different version of the world we lived in, a more spiritual and
meaningful one.

Larisa left us at age 50, two days after her mother's birthday, leaving me with directions on what to buy her mother for a birth-day gift. She was very weak in her last month, but insisted on my taking her to buy a birthday present for our daughter. It was just a few days before she became unconscious.

During treatment she passed the course of Transcendental Meditation, but she never revealed to me her mantra; she kept the promise she gave to her teacher to keep that word a secret.

Larisa always called me "the King of small things," referring to my ability to keep a lot of things under control at once, including the tiniest details. By nature she was a woman of large projects. It took her quite a few years to start believing that I was also capable of creating bigger things. I think if she were alive now, she would make a correction to the title she gave me.

There is no bigger tragedy for any parent than to outlive their children, and despite the deep feelings of loss my children and I experienced, I think Larisa's mother, who had already lost her hus-band a few years earlier, paid the largest toll for that tragic event.

After Larisa's death I faced a new challenge: how to build my relationship with our kids. Now as I became for them both father and mother, I decided to ease up on the pressure they had had be-fore with respect to their studies, the way they spent their time, and the choices they made. In addition to continuing to be a caring and loving parent, the most important task for me was to become their close friend. I think that I achieved that goal and helped my children get through their teenage years with minimal difficulties. We are open with each other and share our lives with each other, and are as close as the Three Musketeers.

To make this happen, I realized that first of all I had to change myself. Life had taught us a cruel lesson and forced me to look at myself from a different angle. The deep transformation I under-went did not happen overnight. It was an intense journey, but now I am quite a different person than I was ten years ago.

First of all I got rid of any type of envy. Some people would probably not believe that this is possible, but now I don't envy any-body or anything. Back in Russia we were raised to always compare ourselves to everyone around us. Mostly such comparisons were focused on career and financial success. Only recently (better late than never!) did I realize that any comparison of ourselves with others does not lead in the right direction but only to envy. Even one of the most standard questions like, "Would you like to be younger?" leaves me indifferent. No, I am happy with exactly where I am today. I also worked to remove from my children's and my vocabulary negative words such as guilt and blame. I believe that any event, even the most tragic one, is a lesson we can learn from, and in this way we can benefit. In every person and every event I try to find only the good, and I believe that the world around us is as we perceive it.

This profound change has brought me to a different state of mind, and I feel more balanced and happier, leading me to the conclusion that happiness simply means that you like living your own life.

As the years pass, I can see how lucky I am in many ways; in particular, with my career and my family. There are days when I feel that I am coming closer to a state of harmony with the world, and at those moments I intuitively feel that there is meaning in life. This fills my heart with warmth and peace.

Life is unquestionably a summation of the choices we've made, and it becomes filled with the events created by those choices. Some of these events we do not like, but once they happen, we have to accept them as a result of our choices and stop rejecting or fighting them. What has happened has happened, and we cannot change it. Resisting the past does not take us anywhere and drains our vital energy that could otherwise be used for something constructive. To be able to turn the negativity of such events into creativity, we have to change our perception, and this is the most important thing we can do for our future. It's about taking charge of our lives.

The power of the mind is immeasurable. Changing one's perception to that of positivity shifts the whole chemistry of our body, and helps us leave the past behind. It will allow us to see, to live in, and appreciate the present moment. Isn't that what we all want?

50 · Remarkable Memories

It's hard to believe that I have played the violin for more than half a century! I would estimate that on average, playing the violin all these years for 3-4 hours a day, my playing time adds up to around 75,000 hours. Thanks to that small fragile instrument, I discovered the thrilling world of classical music. If I had not become a musician, I probably could have become a fashion designer or a chef, but I became a musician, and this allowed my modest life to cross paths with some truly remarkable artists. In over five decades of music making I have met many great musicians. A few left a deep imprint in my memory.

I recall one of the most memorable concerts in Moscow when Vadim Repin, a nine-year-old boy in shorts, a white shirt, and red pioneer tie around his neck performed the Violin Concerto by Russian composer Tikhon Khrennikov with our orchestra (the Moscow State Symphony). Musically the concerto was below average, but it was an extremely virtuosic one. The composer had obviously tried to compensate for his lack of imagination and talent by creating cascades of finger-breaking passages, often artificially constructed. By the time he played with us, Vadim was already a prodigy with the promise of becoming a real musician. He performed on a three-quarter size violin with incredible quality. The young virtuoso brilliantly overcame all of the technical obstacles presented to him. Every note was like a big apple, so tangible and perfect. I have never heard such an incredible young virtuoso in my entire life. Despite this, he was no Jascha Heifetz, but that did not stop him from signing my program many years later as "Jascha." I had the honor of playing with Vadim at the Seattle International Music Festival in 1993. We performed Tchaikovsky's *Souvenir de Florence*, in which I took the second violin part. I still have the program, and prefer to explain Vadim's "Jascha" as an example of his good sense of humor.

I first played with Gunther Herbig in Russia. He conducted an interesting program including Schoenberg's *Transfigured Night*. This piece was neither in the repertoire of the Moscow State Symphony nor any other Russian orchestra. It was very refreshing to play such a powerful piece under the guidance of the distinguished German conductor. I played again with Herbig and the Seattle Symphony two decades later, and he remembered that Moscow concert.

Before our first September rehearsal of the 1998-1999 season and the official opening of Benaroya Hall, a few Seattle Symphony musicians were testing the qualities of the newborn concert hall. I was asked to play in a string quartet for the top orchestra donors to demonstrate how the hall carried the sound of the strings. I remember my first step on the beautifully polished dark hardwood floor of the main auditorium. There was not a single scratch or speck of dust on it. We tuned our instruments, and my violin sounded totally different from how it had sounded in the Opera House, where the Seattle Symphony had performed in previous years. The sound had additional layers of vibrancy and color. It travelled with ease and filled the entire hall. There was no need to press on the bow and force the sound. It was so exciting! I am sure that my colleagues had similar feelings.

A few days later, world famous soprano Jessye Norman made her magnificent debut with the Seattle Symphony at the opening night concert which had sold out months in advance. She walked onstage like a queen; there was something very regal about her presence when she sang the *Immolation Scene* from Wagner's *Gotterdammerung.* Her majestic, dramatic soprano filled not only the hall but also the hearts of everybody who had the good fortune to be present at that concert. Performing the very first concert in the wonderful new hall, for which Seattle had been waiting decades, with the glorious Jessye Norman as soloist was a joyous and ecstatic experience.

Legendary conductor Kurt Masur made an unforgettable impression on the Seattle Symphony musicians and audience alike. He conducted Mozart's Symphony No. 40 and Bruckner's Fourth Symphony. Masur suffered from Parkinson's disease, and his hands shook the entire time. Nevertheless, the Bruckner symphony he conducted created the most magnificent musical cathedral I have ever been in. Sometimes it was hard to understand Masur's beat, but somehow he created a magnetizing field around him, and the orchestra fell under the spell of his mysterious music making.

Thomas Dausgaard was not a newcomer to Seattle. As a Principal Guest Conductor, he had recently brought a cycle of all seven Sibelius symphonies. Not all of these symphonies are of the same quality, and we musicians expressed doubts about the success of that ambitious project. Dausgaard demonstrated a rare ability to transform some not very interesting music into an inspiring performance, and convinced the musicians to trust and follow him. His conducting skills impressed everyone; there was not even one small gesture without meaning or that did not reflect the character he wanted to draw from the music. No wonder Dausgaard won absolute approval from the orchestra. The audience was transfixed, leaping up with standing ovations again and again.

On a couple of occasions, I was asked to play with the Russian National Symphony Orchestra, which performed on tour in Seattle. I had a few friends in the orchestra with whom I had studied and worked back in Moscow. Just a day before coming to Seattle, two orchestra musicians got sick and could not play the concert, and the orchestra needed a substitute. Touring conditions for Russian orchestras have not improved since I left the former Soviet Union, and musicians often got sick because of the stress.

Their Music Director, Mikhail Pletnev, was an internationally acclaimed pianist and a wonderful musician. He came on stage slowly with the score in his left hand. Instantly it grew so quiet that I felt a little chill. It was not just a silence; it was silence with a lot of tension in the air. Tchaikovsky's Fifth Symphony had to be rehearsed. Pletnev put the score on the stand but did not open it. He did not greet the orchestra, and did not look at the musicians. He slowly raised his hands and gave a subtle upbeat.

The music started. I noticed an incredible concentration from the musicians; they were watching their master like hawks. Pletnev's gestures were modest but expressive. He barely moved, but when he did, the orchestra instantly responded with a wave of sound. He did not really look at the musicians either, maybe just an occasional glance toward one section or another. We played through the first movement, then the second and third, without stops or comments from the conductor. In the middle of the Finale, Pletnev suddenly dropped his hands and stopped conducting. Then he gave us a rehearsal letter to start from, and when the orchestra played, he stopped at the same place as before. He slowly raised his head and looked at the first clarinetist. For a few seconds not a word was said. The air was electric. Looking at the musician, Pletnev said in a low voice, "I showed you the entrance the first time, you did not start. I showed you the entrance the second time, you did not start. (Pause.) I hope this will not happen at the concert." The tone of that announcement reminded me of the inquisition times. We finished the glorious Finale; Pletnev picked up the score, did not say a word, slowly stepped down from the podium, and in total silence, left the hall.

The same night at the intermission of the concert a couple of Russian musicians came to me and asked, "Don't you think that he (Pletnev) is a genius?" I was not ready to answer, but they clearly could not imagine an answer that was not a "yes!" I was struck by how much respect and faith they had in their conductor. Most likely he was a genius.

One of the most outstanding opera performances was Wagner's *Tristan and Isolde* in the summer of 1998 with the internationally renowned Swiss conductor, Armin Jordan. He was only 66 years old but he hardly moved, suffering from emphysema. Sitting for the entire five and a half long hours in an armchair, breathing heavily, he mostly cued us with his eyes, but how much meaning there was in those cues! We could not take our eyes off the maestro, and he knew that we would do anything for him. There was so much marvelous music in those performances, so much tenderness and depth.

For many years I had the luck of working with an outstanding composer and extraordinary person, Marvin Hamlisch. He was appointed as the Seattle Symphony Principal Pops Conductor while already holding a similar position with four or five other American orchestras. He was also kind to me and agreed to serve on the Honorary Boards of the Cascade Symphony and the Bellevue Philharmonic.

Hamlisch's extreme popularity was based not only on his wonderful musicals which ran on Broadway for years, but also because he was a man with an unbelievably radiant personality and endless creativity. It took almost nothing for him to make audiences smile. He would come off the podium to the edge of the stage, stare at people, and shrug his shoulders in a typical Jewish gesture of "I know?" That was all it took. The entire hall was smiling. It was so sincere. There was never a shortage of jokes from him. At times they were silly, but always good enough to make the audience roll with laughter. His musical selections, which occasionally included his own music, were exciting and the audience was always happy at his concerts. I can sum up working with Marvin in just one word: fun.

Two legendary musicians disappointed me: Van Cliburn and Isaac Stern. The entire musical world remembered Van Cliburn winning the First Tchaikovsky Competition in Moscow in 1958, despite some resistance from the Russian jury which thought that it would be a disaster for the USSR to give an American the first prize at the most prestigious Russian competition at the height of the Cold War. But everybody in Moscow fell in love with the curly-haired, elegant young fellow from far-away Louisiana. Playing with the Seattle Symphony 40-some years later, Cliburn looked exhausted and his cold playing had no trace of the fire he once produced at the Tchaikovsky competition. It was the performance of a tired man, though he did still have his curly hair, now almost entirely grey.

Isaac Stern was an iconic violinist for me. I had a bunch of his recordings, and one of my favorites was his performance of Lalo's *Symphonie Espagnole* with the Philadelphia Orchestra. This time he played a recital of Brahms Sonatas in the Opera House, and his playing was simply not in tune, which the Seattle Post Intelligencer music critic R. M. Campbell also noted in his review. It's always very hard for a famous concert musician to leave the stage when the time comes, and only a few have had this delicate sense of timing.

Russian pianist Grigory Sokolov won the Gold Medal in the third Tchaikovsky Competition and later grew into an amazing musician with international stature. In my memory, Sokolov performed only once with the Moscow State Symphony, and I can't ever remember playing Tchaikovsky's First Piano Concerto as slowly as we did with him! It was ten minutes longer than other pianists usually played it, but every note had tremendous meaning and the deepest profound musicianship. When a composer writes a piece, he intuitively puts into it a lot of information, which he is actually unaware of. These things happen on a subconscious level. The greatest talents such as Sokolov are able to bring to life such hidden information that others cannot. In this quality lies the "secret" of the genius of the greatest artists we know.

In Lynn Harrell's hands, his cello looked like a three-quarter size. His large hands dwarfed the instrument. Lynn's sound had a special penetrating quality; it went directly to the heart, bypassing the mind. Some of his phrasing was overdone, like slightly overdone steak, but still the voice of his cello stayed remarkably human. I recall the funniest incident when in September, 2005, Harrell played Richard Strauss' *Don Quixote* with the Seattle Symphony. He was waiting for his majestic entrance, and just a few bars before his entrance, we heard the loud and annoying ring of a cell phone. None of the musicians were allowed to take their phones onstage since similar unpleasant incidents had happened in the past when the orchestra was recording. While continuing to play our parts, we looked at each other trying to guess who might be guilty of such a disturbance. The phone rang a second time and we saw Lynn Harrell quickly reach into the inner pocket of his jacket, pull out his phone, shut it down, and drop it back into his pocket and in the next second make his entrance perfectly on time. It was definitely the wrong place but if there was a right time for a phone to ring onstage, then that was it.

Itzhak Perlman was always a hero to me. He had the remarkable ability to translate his positive personality into the warmest tone of his unique instrument, not to mention that he always had a new joke for the musicians.

The playing of Lang Lang was filled with electricity and imagination. He was always very friendly and open. His performances were those of a showman with a sunny personality and incredibly fast fingers, and audiences went crazy at his concerts.

If you think about the most outstanding artistic figures of the 20th century, the name of Mstislav Rostropovich will inevitably come to mind. A great cellist and conductor, he also was a fighter for human rights and freedom. His heroic gesture of protecting the Russian writer Solzhenitsyn cost him many years of "bad luck" from the Russian government, but it did not stop him from doing what he thought was right, and what was so dangerous to do in

Russia at that time.

Rostropovich's charm had no boundaries. Right after finishing a rehearsal he would grab us, his fellow Russian musicians, by the shoulders (and ladies around the waist) and drag us into his room just to share new anecdotes. He enjoyed the company of people so much that his delight was infectious. He behaved as if he had known us for a long time back in Russia when in reality, he had just met us for the first time. He was blessed with the talent of magnetizing people to him and bringing them together. Among friends, this man was down to earth; on stage he was Superman.

I met the outstanding glass artist Dale Chihuly, a longtime generous supporter of the arts in the Pacific Northwest, at one of the parties he threw in his studio in Seattle. It was not a formal party, but musicians from the Seattle Symphony arrived there after the concert, so most of us were dressed in tails. Chihuly was dressed more simply in jeans, a shirt, and sneakers. I noticed that his sneakers were all painted brightly, like somebody had dropped many different colors of paint on them. I was not sure if Dale had come directly from his studio or if he just liked those sneakers. Although his appearance did not match the rest of the company, he did not seem to care. Perhaps he was dressed like that on purpose just to stand out in the crowd as the unique artist he is. I complimented him on his sneakers, saying that they might be sold for a very high price on eBay. He liked the joke, and smiled mysteriously in response. We were offered a private tour of his studio, and it was something really extraordinary: it seemed like Chihuly created a new life using just glass and his endless imagination.

The list of famous people I've had the pleasure of meeting could go on and on.

51 · Concert: Tchaikovsky's Fifth

Let's go backstage with the conductor just before an important concert. From the wings you hear the first oboe sounding an "A." You are a bit nervous. The orchestra is tuning, making that sweet noise which will melt down in a few moments, until the last player is satisfied with the pitch of his or her instrument. The audience stops coughing, and suddenly: silence. They are waiting for you.

You stride onstage and hear applause. You signal for the musicians to rise. Bowing, you turn to the orchestra. Looking at the musicians, you feel their readiness to dive into the drama and beauty of Tchaikovsky's Fifth. You open the score. In a moment you and the musicians will bring to life this masterpiece. You slowly lift your hands and keep them suspended in the air for a couple of seconds. You look directly into the eyes of the clarinets – they will start the main tune of the symphony which you already hear in your head. You give an upbeat while taking a breath with the clarinets. The serious and deep music begins. This is a motif of Fate, a frequent frightening guest in Tchaikovsky's final symphonies. Deeply afraid of Fate, Tchaikovsky tried all his life to avoid it.

You don't move your body at all, only the wrists use the baton to draw in the air a picture of a barely recognizable beat, but you know that the musicians can see and understand it. They are watching at this very moment the tip of your baton, which indicates what character of music you want them to create. You don't move your body, and remain focused on the clarinets, continuing to direct their melody. The musicians read the diagram that the tip of your baton is drawing, and in these gestures are all the information they need: rhythm, tempo, dynamics, and most importantly, the color of the sound. Dark and mysterious.

Your head doesn't move and the expression on your face does not change until the strings slowly emerge, and then when the time is right, with a subtle turn of the head you invite the strings to support the clarinets. They must be gentle so as not to overpower the still soloing clarinets. It's not easy for fifty string players to play softer than two clarinets, but that is how it should be, how the composer wrote it to be.

Step by step, the strings slowly rise in volume and gradually take over. They are now leading the melody, and the clarinets can relax a bit: their mellow sound has already melted into the strong mezzo-forte of the strings. The whole orchestra is awakened now and you have to tame this giant and put him on a leash while simultaneously gaining the giant's trust. Without his trust, no leash in the world will be strong enough to hold him back.

Now your eyes move from one group of instruments to another, depending on their importance at that particular moment. The drama builds. The expression on your face changes, it shows the more intense character of the music you want to draw from the orchestra. Your gestures become bigger, more energetic, but they do not lose their clarity. You feel the electricity accumulating around you: the music approaches its climax.

You can see the eyes of all 80 musicians gazing intently at you. They await your signal so that they can bring the music to its powerful climax. Your gestures continue to become more and more intense, your body accumulates energy, your eyes radiate power, and with the strongest, widest gesture you can muster, the whole orchestra explodes. Nothing can contain its energy.

It's as if this swell of sound has destroyed all that has come before it, and everything must now be rebuilt from the ground up. Everyone is out of breath. We take a moment to recharge before moving on.

There is so much more pain and despair in the second movement. It is a story of unrequited love, or perhaps of love that was never found. Every note in this autobiographical symphony tells us something about the composer's life.

Third movement. Our hero tries to escape the cruel reality of his Fate through the dreams of the *Valse*. What lies ahead?

The Finale's dark motif turns into the frightening call of Fate, and then unexpectedly takes on a major key, demonstrating the triumphal march of Life. Is this a victory or just a ray of hope? The orchestra glows with bright sound, and then without any warning you take an impossibly fast tempo in the coda finale. You see the musicians moving to the edge of their chairs, they are giving more than they ever had. Your excitement and energy is so infectious; you are now becoming one with the orchestra. The conductor and musicians have vanished; only a trembling ball of energy remains.

The magnificent symphony ends with four notes in the major key: ta-ta-ta-TA! – the same famous rhythm that opens Beethoven's Fifth Symphony. It is Fate, knocking at the door. Beethoven wrote these four notes in 1808, and 80 years later the same motif would haunt and possess Tchaikovsky as he wrote his own Fifth Symphony. Fate became an equal obsession for both composers.

Five years later, Tchaikovsky's triumphant march of life would be followed by the most depressing music ever written: the finale of his Symphony No. 6, the famous *Pathetique*. The Fate that loomed over Tchaikovsky all his life would finally win, ushering in the finale of the remarkable and tragic life of one of the greatest Russian composers of all time.

52 · A "Master" Around Every Corner

When I was growing up in Russia during the 60s and 70s, a period in which the Soviet Union and America were pretending to be on friendly terms, there was a notion that Russian and American people were very similar in that they were both very open and affable. (This meant, of course, that it was the vicious American government that later led the two countries to become enemies during the Cold War.) Thirty-five years of living in Russia and twenty-five in America have provided me with enough perspective to look at that time with a certain objectivity, and has led me to realize that this was one of the biggest propagated lies. Upon coming to America, I realized that Russians and Americans couldn't be more different.

The eyes of a human being reflect his or her spirit, and it is freedom that radiates from an American's eyes as much as it is a lack thereof in the eyes of a Russian. No one can blame them for that. Russia was historically ruled by a czar, and after the Bolshevik revolution it became a totalitarian society built on the same principles. Hundreds of years of living under a czar and totalitarianism left Russian people with a sort of imprisonment complex.

After 1990 when communism began to crumble, there was finally hope that freedom might come to Russian society and change its people for the better. However, only a few years later the economy became even worse than before, leading the majority of Russian people to declare that they no longer cared about freedom. They just wanted to see bread on the table. It is so sad that even now, many Russians are still brainwashed by government propaganda and still think of America as they did during the height of the Cold War. In total contrast to Russia, America was built on the principle of freedom, and it has become a cornerstone in the mentality of society that makes all the difference in fostering a feeling of independence and undefeatable pride.

As an older country, Russia's culture is also much older than America's. In many ways this is a huge privilege, but I've found it's also important to take into consideration the "everyday" culture of a society. Whereas Russians aren't afraid to push you when standing in line or passing you on the street, Americans will give you plenty of room and apologize profusely if they jostle you. Whereas Russians would never greet anyone on the street except for someone they knew, Americans will greet you with a smile even if you are a stranger. Whereas when Russians get drunk and angry they could easily hit you in the face without much thought, Americans tend to want to avoid confrontation at all costs. Whereas Russians don't consider stealing from their country (workplace, etc.) a bad thing, Americans are raised to respect another's property. If you think Americans swear a lot, visit Russia! There is a whole separate lexicon in Russian designated to cursing. Russians can engage in an entire conversation using only curse words and still express their feelings completely without adding a single "normal" word! In some ways this is quite impressive, but in others it is quite sad.

There is a popular Russian anecdote that goes like this: a tourist in Moscow takes a cab and notices that the driver makes sudden stops at green lights while running every red light. "Why are you doing that?" asks the passenger. "You're doing it backwards!" The cab driver responds, "There's a 'master' around every corner." (That probably does not make much sense translated into English, but it means that one cannot be too careful – crazy drivers can be lurking around every corner.) Anecdotes often shed light on the mentality of society. Beyond the direct translation of this anecdote is something that explains what lies at the root of Russian character: they do not like to follow rules. It's not that Russians totally reject authority, but when it comes to everyday life they cannot live without breaking rules. This cultural acceptance of doing things upside down and inside out affects the mind on a deep level.

Two of the most common expressions I hear in America are "you never know" and "to be in the right place at the right time." This is profound wisdom most Americans take for granted; to me it is an invaluable gift. In Russia we always knew how everything was going to be and did not expect surprises from everyday life. We knew what we would find in the store (or rather, what we would not find in the store), and what our future would be. In America, the country of constant change, each morning when you leave the house you take "you never know" with you as you would carry an umbrella in case of rain. Be prepared for the unexpected. Yes, it keeps you on your toes, but that's how life here works. It also means I might learn something new every day; I just don't know when and where it will be.

And as for being in the right place at the right time, I like to think that America is the right place for me, and the time is now and for the rest of my life.

Eternity

Listening to music is always an intimate process. Whether in a concert hall with 2,000 other listeners, or in a small room holding the hand of your sweetheart, you are always left one on one with your feelings. On the contrary, playing in the orchestra gives you a feeling of being a part of a team in which your emotions are carried in a huge wave, and mix with the emotions of fellow musicians.

I consider classical music concerts to be one of the highest forms of healthy pleasure we can find in our lives. The effect of the live vibration in the concert hall is incomparable to any other human activity. Perhaps the emotion of an exciting sporting event can come close, but not on a spiritual level.

Reading great books or attending an art exhibition can educate us and give us spiritual pleasure. But only in the concert hall can you have it all: the experience of physical, educational, emotional, and spiritual uplift. This is why I believe that the symphony orchestra is the highest form of human cultural achievement.

Classical music is like a layer cake. Because of this, people with all different levels of exposure to and knowledge of the art form can enjoy it. Listening to music you will find the "layer" you like the most and the one that speaks to you. You don't need to know much to come to the concert hall and enjoy a musical evening; you learn as you go. Listening over and over to a piece of classical music might be similar to visiting an art museum and circling Michelangelo's David or seeing the Mona Lisa for the hundredth time; no viewing is the same. With every exposure, the listener (or viewer) takes away new meaning, noticing subtleties that went undiscovered in the previous sessions. Great art opens up our minds to endless interpretation. It awakens our imagination and creativity, coaxing open our very souls, which can be so stifled by modern life.

Spoken language is open to so many misinterpretations and can be so deceptive. What is supposed to become the main communicative tool in human history often becomes instead the main tool in human misunderstanding. Music, on the other hand, is a tool of communication far more perfect than language. It's absolutely universal, and it doesn't require any sort of special preparation. When it is good, everybody feels it instantly. Music was given to us so that we can better communicate with each other on a higher level of consciousness.

The role of art is to keep us human, and remind us of who we really are: a unique creation of nature, with unparalleled ability to create and grow. In my view, great music is part of a plan to prevent us humans from exterminating each other. Every time we play or every time we hear music, we communicate directly to this higher consciousness.

And now let me ask you: how many times in a lifetime will you re-read your favorite novel? Ten? Probably less than that. But why don't we get tired of listening to the same musical piece dozens and dozens, if not hundreds of times? Why do we want to hear Handel's "Messiah," Beethoven's Ninth Symphony, or Mozart's "Eine kleine Nachtmusik," again and again?

The fine arts, especially classical music, can be compared to a river. An old proverb says, "One cannot step in the same river twice." Similarly, one cannot perform or approach the same musical piece the same way twice. Every musical masterpiece contains a well of information that cannot be measured or completely described.

Appreciation of music requires human contact – interaction and participation – and here is where unpredictability enters, since we are never the same. We change constantly without even recognizing that we have changed. We are different each time we wake up, each time we breathe, and each time we listen to Beethoven's "Eroica."

The unique complexity of human beings, which is absolutely impossible to describe now or ever in the future, makes contact with the complexity of the musical piece we are in the process of experiencing. Each time we feel the same music differently because each time we travel into different "pockets" of information; the whole process of such interaction becomes unique and cannot be copied or repeated. Such undetectable fluctuation between us and a great work of music can only be compared to the fluctuation of the stock market on a very busy day. That's why we will never exhaust the endless possibilities of enjoying classical music. The more information the musical piece contains, and the more experience the listener brings to it, the more possibilities for the interpretation and perception it creates. It's one of the life forms that had a beginning, but has no end.

Closing Note

Dear Reader,

Thank you very much for making the effort to read about my life and making it to this page. (I will not be offended if you skipped some.)

When I came to America, it was like emerging from the Stone Age. Back in Russia we often joked about the meaning of certain words. The Soviet Union translates to "Sovietskiy Soyuz." The word "Sovietskiy" is derived from "Soviet," which also means "advice." We called our country "The country of soviets (or advice)." In a moment you will see where I am going.

In America I learned that I have to ask for advice when I need it, but should not give advice if people do not ask for it. In Russia everybody gives constant advice to everybody on everything. This is part of the culture. In the words of a popular Russian anecdote: "Why can't one have sex in the middle of Moscow's Red Square? Because he will be bombarded with advice on how to do it!"

Since I cannot completely overcome my Russian nature, I will leave you with a small piece of advice. (I know you are not asking for it.) Please close this book, unless you have enough patience to read one more chapter. For some time you have lived with me and my life. It is time now to get back to yours. Each moment is precious. Find and pursue your own dream. In this country, you can.

End of Part Two

Maestro, Play On
by Dale Burrows

"If music be the food of love, play on."
—Shakespeare, *Twelfth Night*

As a little boy, it was the violin; as a young man, it was the baton; and today, he sits with the Seattle Symphony Orchestra as Assistant Principal Second Violin and stands before the Cascade Symphony Orchestra as Music Director and Conductor.

The facts of Michael Miropolsky's life read like a Cinderella story: born in 1955, Bishkek, Kyrgyzstan, Soviet Union; singled out at age thirteen for a musical education through college at state expense because of perfect pitch, memory for music and sense of rhythm; audited classes in conducting after college and toured twenty five countries over ten years with the Moscow State Symphony as Assistant Principal Second Violin; immigrated to San Francisco in 1990; signed with the Seattle Symphony and relocated here a year and a half later.

However, read between the lines.

Uprooting from his family home to a school in Moscow was a condition of the scholarship that educated Miropolsky. Satisfying that condition meant picking up a small town boy from everything he knew and setting him down in a big city, alone, on his own and under uncompromising pressure to perform. That is a big load for small shoulders.

Years later, during the Soviet Union's collapse, the KGB blocked Miropolsky and his wife's petition to emigrate. The block lifted eventually; but in the meantime, persecution for being Jewish in a time of social chaos must have kept him and his wife in a state of high anxiety. Then, a month after arriving in San Francisco with his pregnant wife, this man of music transformed into a family man in a strange city with a wife and baby daughter to support and only his violin to make a living.

"There is too much competition," a lady acquaintance said. "Go into computers." The lady made sense. Nonetheless, "Practicing violin" was Miropolsky's answer six months later when the lady asked him what he had been doing. She had tested his resolve, and he had passed her test. A year later, with that same lady's help, Miropolsky and his violin were providing for his family here in Seattle.

Since then, Miropolsky has conducted the Seattle Violin Virtuosi, Seattle Chamber Orchestra and Bellevue Philharmonic Orchestra besides recording at least ten CDs with his American groups. He has sat with various committees that influence music locally, taught and continues to teach.

To date, Miropolsky has endured the loss of his dear wife, finished raising their daughter and son, maintains close ties with both, and keeps a busy schedule. When asked how he manages his time, "Balance" was the watchword Miropolsky used to point out the star he steers by.

Balance?

I have seen what this man can do with only a baton in his hand, standing before some eighty plus musicians seated with their instruments and surrounding him on three sides. From dead silence, I have seen him, like a magician with his magic wand generate a rising tide of passions in turmoil up off the pages of the score before him until the Cascade Symphony Orchestra flooded all of the Edmonds Center for the Arts with the living presence of Rachmaninoff.

A feat like that must come from within. It takes concentration of will and leaves the one who performed it drained dry of what he has to give.

How, possibly, after something like that, can Miropolsky even hope to restore himself to any kind of equilibrium?

Sunning on the deck of his backyard and walking Green Lake had put him in a light, bright mood when we talked over cell phones on two occasions.

Time alone no doubt contributes to his peace of mind.

Pride without ego and contentment textured the tone of his voice when Miropolsky mentioned neither his daughter nor his son is following in his footsteps professionally. She graduates this year with a major in psychology, and he starts college this year with a major in computer science; both career choices made by them and respected by their father. What makes his kids happy makes Miropolsky happy.

Family of course is fundamental to any centered human being.

Miropolsky moved easily among the musicians he works with and their families at the annual potlucks CSO included me in. His manner was polite, pleasant, familiar but not too familiar. He enjoyed himself.

Food was the surprise.

The clue came when Miropolsky lit up like a Christmas tree promoting the book of recipes with selections of classical music that CSO put together, published, and sells: *Measures and Pleasures* is the title. Food to prepare, food to dine with and music to listen to while preparing and dining: "Food and music go together," Miropolsky announced his version of the truth that must follow as the night the day. Well, I have broken bread with him, heard his music, and my version of the truth is: For Michael Miropolsky, food and music are essential to love of life; he has a big appetite for both; and his sense of play goes everywhere he goes.

Maestro, play on.

2012

Photo Album: America

Violin Ensemble at the Seattle Conservatory of Music

*Program cover for the Jewish Community Center
New Chamber Orchestra*

*Poster of the first concert of the Seattle Violin Virtuosi
at Benaroya Hall in 1999*

*Postcard for the Seattle Chamber
Orchestra concert*

Seattle Violin Virtuosi postcard

Cover for the Seattle Violin Virtuosi's CD
"America, the Beautiful"

At home working on arrangements for the Seattle Violin Virtuosi

Having fun at the Cascade Symphony Orchestra Gala

*The Cascade Symphony Orchestra musicians'
edible gift to me*

*Cover for Cascade Symphony's
collaborative project with Rick
Steves' "Europe, A Symphonic
Journey"*

With Rick Steves at the Cascade Symphony Gala

*With the founder of the Cascade Symphony Orchestra,
Robert Anderson*

With composer Charles-Henri Avelange and his wife Jennifer at the 38th Seattle International Film Festival's Opening Night. The Bellevue Philharmonic performed his Overture at McCaw Hall, in 2012

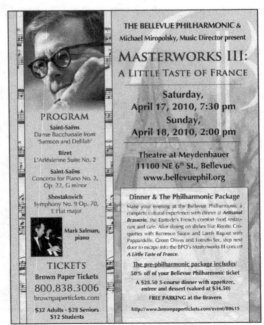

Program cover of the Bellevue Philharmonic Orchestra

*Program cover for the Lake Washington
Symphony Orchestra concert "The Planets"*

Program cover for Thalia Symphony Orchestra

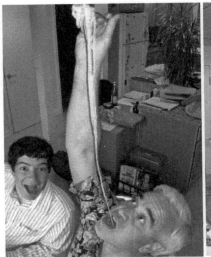

Testing a new "superpasta" recipe

Creating an exotic pineapple recipe

With my son Alex at the annual Cascade Symphony potluck

With euphonium virtuoso Adam Frey

With actress Shirley MacLaine

With the legendary Itzhak Perlman

With composer John Adams

With renowned composer Marvin Hamlisch

With Russian violinist Vadim Repin at the Seattle International Music Festival

With Washington State Governor Gary Locke

With Bill Gates

*My daughter and I with Russian pianist
Evgeny Kissin*

Larisa and I with Mstislav Rostropovich

With Ron Woodard (left), and Althea and Samuel Stroum

Larisa and I with Russian violinist Vladimir Spivakov

*With Russian violinist
Maxim Vengerov*

*With Russian conductor
Vassily Sinaisky*

If you would like to order another copy of this book, please send $25 US for each book (this includes shipping within the US only). Please include check or money order with your name and return address, and send to:

Michael Miropolsky
2943 25th Ave. West
Seattle, WA 98199 USA

Your name and address:

Name_____

Address_____

City_____ State_____ Zip_____

Phone_____

Email _____
(Optional - will not be shared)

If you have comments, please send them to the address above, or email them to: mmiropolsky@comcast.net.

You can also purchase the book from the Seattle Symphony "Symphonica" store at the Benaroya Hall in Seattle, or from Amazon.com (also available in Kindle version).